THE BEST OF AL CLOUSTON

A Collection of Uncle Al's
Best Yarns From The Stateheads
of Newfoundland

Manufactured in Canada by Webcom Limited

ISBN 0-9693723-2-9

Published 1994 by
Al Clouston Publications
P.O. Box 5922
St. John's, Nfld., A1C 5X4

DEDICATION

Again we must be true to the people who molded this island's love of fun.

So we say the same as we said before, this book is dedicated to all humourous characters of Newfoundland past and present, who without knowing it made life bearable. They did this through their unconscious production of fun which is good for body and soul.

Who said it is not always known, but how better can we remember them than to record these contributions for generations, present and future to enjoy.

FOREWORD

Al Clouston listens, he remembers and he repeats.

It sounds like the simplest thing in the world to do but it is really a fine art.

The proof of how well he has mastered this art lies in the remarkably few complaints there are about his work from that most critical audience, the very Newfoundlanders he talks or writes about. I have never heard a single one.

We Newfoundlanders can be touchy as boils. We have good reason to be. For years, we have suffered the abominable curse of "Newfie Jokes" and a feeling of being sneered at by others.

So even real, genuine true-blue, real-life Newfoundland stories can draw attack if there is the faintest suggestion of mean mockery, condescension or ill will in them. The slightest slip can bring a ton of bricks down on you. Lord knows, I know.

But Al Clouston never slips. He manages this by being an honest, simple and straightforward recorder of real Newfoundland stories and jokes. No one can say of his work, "He's making fun of us!" because these are the same stories we tell about ourselves.

He also handles our various dialects or accents well, putting in just enough to add to the flavour of the story but is never tempted to overdo or parody the unique styles of Newfoundland speech.

He's doing what many of us wish we had done or could do . . . creating a permanent record of a Newfoundland long said to be in danger of fading away.

But there's been too much dreary prophesying about our "dying culture" our "vanishing customs" our "disappearing ways". Newfoundlanders don't kill that easily. Our stories and our songs and our ways will never be swamped beneath a tide of somebody else's culture as long as there are Al Cloustons to naturally and honestly breathe new life into them and discover new stories created only yesterday.

He is a storyteller in the best of our old tradition and a good ambassador for us in these new times.

Ray Guy

INTRODUCTION

THE BEST OF AL CLOUSTON. The humourous stories in this book have been taken from my four books of Newfoundland folklore humour.

In 1975 I published my first record, "SPINNIN' YARNS". During that year I was in Toronto and was interviewed by Barbara Frum on "As It Happens". One day I went to the C.B.C. studio of that radio program and placed three records on the counter and left. My phone number was on the outside of the package. I said, "If that's good humour they will call me". At three o'clock I got that call and they requested that I come to the studio right then. The interview was a very pleasant one. Barbara made you feel at ease immediately. Near the end of the interview Barbara said, "Al, I have read about New-foundlanders and the hard time they had through the centuries eking a living out of the North Atlantic. I guess what I am saying is, if life is tough the best thing you can do is laugh at it".

You see it began a long time ago when isolation made us a self-reliant people. Each community dealing with its own problems and overcoming all phases of the tough life of living off the sea, and doing it with lots of fun thrown in. What a wise comment by Barbara just by reading about us.

At the Canadian Managing Editors Conference in St. John's in 1977 I was guest speaker. After he heard me speak and tell some of our folklore humour stories, Ray Timson, Managing Editor of the Toronto Star said to me, "Al, the wit and humour which I heard you tell today is the most original I have heard for a long time. Do you know why?" I said, "You tell me Ray." His reply, "Nobody stayed up half the night dreaming it up." What a comment? Nothing could be closer to the truth.

This humour I call circumstantial humour. The circumstances have to exist and someone of the actors has to think quickly to create the punch line. I do not take any credit for the stories I tell. In some strange way, the most original wit and humour is produced from everyday living, and it is some unknown quick witted character who says it.

To go further, I believe that our forefathers knew subconsciously that humour is a food of living. They knew also that they had to make it themselves. By reason of lack of transportation groups did not move from community to community offering entertainment. So each created its own.

People like the Newfoundlander's distinctive humour. Laughter here in Newfoundland has always been as essential as bread and butter; it's part of living, it's made every day. Newfoundland humour is the type that pokes fun at ourselves and at one another. In other words, laughing at ourselves and others without hurting anybody.

I hasten to add once more that I don't take credit for any of it. My talent is only in the telling of it and then publishing our folklore humour for all to enjoy.

Al Clouston

TRY IT AGAIN!

I have found that when Newfoundlanders are present at mainland functions, it is quite normal for speakers to use a couple of Newfie Jokes to get a laugh. This happens mostly in Ontario and Quebec.

The only defence to this kind of treatment is to throw similar treatment back. In other words, give as good as is sent to you. Here is one experience I had personally.

In 1970, the Lennox Industries Inc. held in Toronto a two-day meeting of all its dealers. Being a Lennox dealer, I travelled to Toronto to attend this meeting.

At one of the luncheons, a Mr. Shipp gave a talk about the construction industry in general. At the luncheon there was about three hundred people. I had never met Mr. Shipp but right in the middle of his speech, and for no reason at all, he told this story.

"I was down to Al Clouston's country and representatives of the industry met me at the airport, gave me a tour of St. John's, installed me in the Newfoundland Hotel and when we got to the room, we ordered up some mix and ice cubes. Up came the mix but no ice cubes. We phoned down to see why no ice cubes and they told us the old lady who made the ice cubes had died two weeks ago and taken the recipe with her." As you can imagine, the story produced a great laugh.

However, when the luncheon was over, I went up to my good friend, Mr. Ray Robbins, manager of Lennox Industries, and asked him to introduce me to Mr. Shipp. Mr. Robbins said, "We told him, Al, if he used your name, he would get it back ten fold."

I was introduced to Mr. Shipp and after a few comments said, "Mr. Shipp, did you hear about the coast guard captain who was sailing around our Newfoundland shores last summer?" He said, "No, what about him?" I continued, "Well, he was feeling a bit mischievous this afternoon, and seeing a lone fisherman in a dory about two miles off shore, stopped his engines and taking his megaphone, he engaged the fisherman in conversation.

CAPTAIN: Do you know you are fishing in Canadian waters?

FISHERMAN: Yis, zar.

CAPTAIN: Do you know you are catching Canadian fish?

FISHERMAN: No, zar.

CAPTAIN: There's a lot of fish there in the bow of your boat. What are they?

FISHERMAN: Dem's Newfoundland fish, zar.

CAPTAIN: How do you know them apart?

FISHERMAN: *We t'rows back d'ones wid d'big mout's.*

COULDN'T DAMPEN THEIR SPIRITS

Two Newfoundlanders decided they had had enough of Toronto and decided to quit their jobs and go back home to start fishing again.

To save money they also decided to hitch-hike. They made their way to the highway and were quite successful in getting rides right to Nova Scotia in two days.

On the third day two men with a pick-up truck stopped and offered them a lift but they would have to get in the box behind because there was only enough room in the cab for two. That was O.K. with the two Newfoundland boys and up they got in the box.

Some time in the afternoon the pick-up went off the road and plunged into a deep lake. The two men in the cab got out and came to the surface and swam to shore.

When there was no sign of the Newfoundlanders coming to the surface after five minutes, the owner became worried and said to his friend that they had better notify the authorities of a drowning accident.

But just then the Newfoundlanders broke the surface of the water and swam to shore. When they waded ashore the owner of the pick-up said to them, "What kept you two fellows so long?", and one of them answered, "We had a tuff job b'y, gettin' the tailgate down."

FRESH AIR

A few years back pollution in Canada was getting the headlines a little more than it is today. Toronto and Montreal were receiving most of the attention.

On one occasion about this time, a Torontonian arrived at Torbay Airport in Newfoundland, via Air Canada, and was walking down the gangway from the plane. He was sniffing all the way down and when he arrived at the bottom of the gangway he said to the attendant, "What's that strange smell I'm getting?" The attendant replied, "Don't worry about that, ol' man, that's only fresh air."

Years ago cobblers had a great trade going. There wasn't a lot of money around so people used to get as much go out of dem boots as dey could get. One day ol' Leo heads to town wit d'saddest lookin' pair of boots you see . . . Up to d'cobbler eh goes . . .

MOTHER BURKE

At the foot of Cape John stands a tall rock shaped like a woman wrapped in a shawl—Mother Burke—now immortalized forever in stone.

When travelling on the *S.S. Prospero* I always wanted to see "Mother Burke" as I had heard so much talk about the same, and each time the weather didn't cooperate. I wasn't very old at the time but was fascinated by this phenomenon nevertheless. So it was years later that I got a chance to see Mother Burke from the top deck of the *S.S. Northern Ranger* on my way to St. John's.

There was then something on the top of this tall rock—people said a Frenchman had scaled it one time and planted a cross there. Others said it was a lantern, but whatever it was it had then fell into disrepair. And so the stories went. I have heard so many I hardly know where to begin.

Years gone by, the clergy used to explain such things as people put back on earth to do penance that was left undone while on earth. Mother Burke was one such soul, I guess, and she sure got around.

To the best of my knowledge, she was first seen at Conche. Then fishermen on the small Grey Island called "Northern Island" reported seeing her, until one fine spring morning before the fishing season opened, two men from the big Grey Island went out there to "Noder Island", as they called it and which is only five miles away.

This day after spending time ashore (there were a few fishermen's shacks on the tiny island), they boarded their skiff to head for home. As they pushed off from the rocks at McGrath's Cove, the only cove on the entire island, their boat dipped by the prow as if someone had stepped on board with them. After this, she was seen on the big Grey Island where all the livyers were.

One evening two small children fell asleep in the hayfield. Soon after they ran crying to their mother that they were awakened by a tall lady wrapped in a huge black shawl. She had been standing over them as they woke up and they were terrified.

Then one night later the same fall, a dance was in progress in a house over at French Cove. It being a muggy night, one of the men went outdoors to cool off after his time on the dance floor. As he was standing there in the cool night air, a tall figure passed by so startling him that he used some very strong language. Inside the house people said they heard a woman scream, but outside he had heard nothing. But, as he came to think about this after, he realized the figure that passed by him was wrapped in a shawl which was very odd for such a warm night. Thus he knew he had seen Mother Burke.

In my own time, stories of her were still told and we even played a game as children and called it "Old Mother Burke" with one of us wrapped in a shawl.

Jean Hurley
Grey Islands

DERM DUGGAN

5

BUNK OUT WITH STRANGERS

The lady said this story is true and it is believable for sure.

Five years ago my husband had a summer job at Churchill Falls. I decided I would visit with him for a few days. On the plane I sat near a lady who was also heading for Churchill Falls. Her husband had a summer job too.

Just before we were to land at Churchill Falls an announcement came over the P.A. that it was too foggy to land and we would land at Goose Bay for overnight.

We were taken to the Goose Hotel, there was thirteen of us. The clerk of the hotel informed us that there was a shortage of rooms, and she asked if some of us would "double up". I readily agreed that I would share a room with my new found friend.

The room to which we were assigned had only one double bed. As we got ready to "bunk it out", I started to laugh. My friend looked bewildered and said, "what's so funny?" I replied, "y'know when I was a girl my mother told me not to get in cars with strangers . . . she should see me now . . . I'm getting in bed with one."

CHURCH STREET AND ISLAND COVE

Two Island Cove chaps went to Toronto to get jobs. They were successful, but to get to the site of the construction, they had to ride the buses and transfer a few times. Getting home, the routine was the same. One day, for some reason, the bus which they would normally use to get home did not show up at the time that it did on other days. They were not taking a chance on taking another bus for fear of getting lost.

They waited nearly two hours, and when a bus stopped by them, one of them stepped aboard and asked the driver some questions. He then leaned out of the bus and yelled to his buddy: "Billy, this one is going to church. (Church Street) The reply came back, "I don't care now if she's goin' to Sunday School, were goin' to take 'er."

6

A LONG DAY'S NIGHT

For years a man had taken time out to go on a booze for himself for a month or so. As he got older he found he wanted to linger a little longer with the stuff and a month became two months before he would sober up.

On one of these longer trips he was sitting outside on the back of his house one morning. It was a beautiful sunny day but our friend couldn't determine what time of day it was. You have heard the remark, "He was so drunk for so long he didn't know night from day." Well this is where he was.

On this particular day he felt there was someone sitting near him and slowly raising his hand and glancing skywards and with a very thick tongue, said,

COMMON ASSAULT $25.00

There are many stories told about our courts regarding the decision of Magistrates and their peculiarities. One Magistrate about whom I was told, said, he only heard one side of any case, because if he heard both sides he got confused.

However, years ago there was a standard fine meted out to all offenders who were guilty of common assault. This fine was $25.00.

I can vouch for this particular incident. A fight broke out between two men who had not been on altogether good terms for years. It appears that the wives of each were backing her man, come what may. Those who tried to patch up the quarrel were politely told to mind their own business.

One afternoon it came to fisty-cuffs and the two wives were sent for. When it was very evident that one of the men was losing badly, his wife yelled to him, "Gisen d'boots, Garge, I got $25.00."

LET 'ER SLIDE

In a small community on our island, most people went to church. To get to the church, it was necessary to climb a steep hill. In winter the children used this hill for randying and on this Sunday in particular, the hill was nuttin' but a glare.

After church, an old man was giving an elderly woman a hand down the hill when he slipped and she fell smack on top of him.

Well down the hill they went lickety split. They went clear to the bottom where they struck a big tree. The old fellow looked up at the old lady, still lying across him, and said, "You're going to have to get off now, cuz this is as far as I'm going. No charge."

PAID FER UT

The Rev. George Earle is one of Newfoundland's best entertainers with what he calls "Newfoundlandia". He told the following story at one function I attended.

A clergyman was gently chiding one of his old parishoners about his non-attendance at church on Sunday.

NEWFOUNDLANDERS

During the war boom in Newfoundland, American foremen and superintendents were appalled that a man would leave a good job, just to be at home for a few months. There was moose huntin' and birdin' to be done too. These Americans did not know that Newfoundlanders "went home in the fall."

An Irishman, an American and a Newfoundlander all arrived at the gate of heaven at the same time. St. Peter addressed the Irishman first and asked his nationality. He was told to take the first train north and he would get to the community where all the Irishmen were congregated. St. Peter directed the American to take the next train south.

When St. Peter came to the Newfoundlander he said "Where do you belong?"

"Newfoundland," was the reply. And St. Peter said, "My son you'd better stay right here by the gate because you'll want to go home in the fall."

A FAST COURTSHIP

One day Nicholas Schenck, movie millionaire, about to board Tom Meighan's yacht, saw a slip of a girl standing on the edge of the wharf.

"For some inexplicable reason," Mr. Schneck recalls, "I had an uncontrollable impulse to push her into the water. To my horror I did. I had no idea if she could swim. I expected an infuriated young woman. Instead, she came to the surface, blinked the water out of her eyes and smiled a brilliant smile.

"By God!" I said to myself, "that's the girl I'm going to marry!" And he did.

NO DOUBT EMBARRASSING

A kind and humble priest in our island had been in the parish of a rural district for many years. He was looked upon almost as a part of every family in the parish. He knew them all by their first names because he had christened most of them and saw them grow up. He was truly respected and loved. This affection was in return for the care and kindness he had shown his parishioners.

On one occasion however, an area of his humility backfired slightly. From time to time a new housekeeper was engaged and in his desire to have them feel a part of his household, he told each one not to refer to things about the residence as his but 'our'. For instance, they were to refer to the cooking stove, the refrigerator, or carpet as 'our' not 'your'.

This particular day the priest had a fellow priest in his study when the rather young housekeeper carried this "our" business, in her excitement, a bit too far. She rushed into the study out of breath and exclaimed,

"OH FATHER FATHER THERES A MOUSE UNDER OUR BED!"

IT WAS A BERRY FUNNY TING

Since this is berry-picking time, I think I should tell the story of years ago when only a small percentage of the people in Newfoundland were literate.

In those days, the department of communications was called The Postal Telegraphs. It received its name from the fact that the individual in the community who had the post office also had to be a telegraph operator.

What would happen was this: The people of the community who could not write would get others to write a letter for them and place it in the envelope and the postmaster or postmistress would address it for them.

One day a fellow brought a box to the post office, to be sent in the mail, and the postmaster addressed it for him. . .

Postmaster: "Who's the parcel going to?"

Sender: "John Burry, 10 Carter's Hill, St. John's."

Postmaster: "Who's the sender?"

Sender: "Bill Burry."

Postmaster: "What's in the parcel?"

Sender: "BURRIES!"

DERM DUGGAN

12

LOCAL DOINGS MORE IMPORTANT

During the second World War, a crew of Americans were engaged cutting a line across Newfoundland. Another crew would eventually follow and their job would be to cut the right of way.

The first crew had gotten well ahead of those to follow. One evening one of these American chaps visited a remote settlement on the coast. He wished to use a telephone but there was no telephone there and he was informed also that there was no telegraph station. He went into a store to buy some newspapers but none were available.

When he came out, he noticed some people standing on the bridge further down the road, so he walked down and joined them. The American asked some questions about the locality and eventually made this observation,

"THIS IS A GOD-FORSAKEN PLACE. YOU DONT HAVE ANY TELEPHONES, OR TELEGRAPH STATIONS. YOU CANT EVEN BUY A NEWSPAPER HERE. YOU PEOPLE DONT KNOW WHAT WE ARE DOING UP IN PLACES LIKE NEW YORK, BOSTON, OR CHIGAGO."

"NO ME ZON. AN'NIDER DO YOUSE FELLERS KNOW WHAT WEEM DOIN' DOWN YER."

THE CENTRE BALL

All through the 1940's, I was a member of the executive of the St. John's Kinsmen Club. Each year we had visits from district governors and sometimes representatives from the national executive.

On one occasion, and this was the only time it happened, a visiting governor arrived who had been overindulging, but who, with our help, overcame that hazard by the next afternoon. We were quite happy about this. However, by 7 o'clock, the time for the public function, our governor had indulged himself a little too much again. When it came his turn to speak he surprised us by not doing too badly.

We learned afterwards that it must have been the advice he was given by Judge Billy Higgins, our guest speaker who spoke before our governor.

Before Judge Higgins finished speaking, he noticed our visiting delegate and gave him some advice by telling a story. He said, "Now, look here, Governor John. I want to give you a little advice. When I was a young fella about eighteen years of age, I was captain of the B.I.S. football team. Now we had for a goalkeeper a chap by the name of Mike. Sometimes he would appear at 7 o'clock but was not altogether in proper state of health to tend goal and we would have to substitute him and use a spare fella who was always about.

On this particular evening, Mike was in a very poor state of health. The bottle had got to him again. But our spare was nowheres about. Well, it was a championship game and what were we going to do? We had to have eleven men on the field, so we decided to tell Mike if he would only lean against the goal and not move it would be ok. We warned our two full-backs to play goal as well as their own positions. By gosh, everything went fine. We were playing the Methodist Guards and at half time we had scored one goal and the Guards none.

In the second half, everything went fine until two minutes before the game came to an end, when the Guards broke through and it had to be a sure goal. But what do you know? Just as the ball was going over the goal line, our friend Mike came to life, grabbed the ball and threw it to one side. The game ended and we had won and I went over to our goalkeeper and said,

'Mike, how did you save that ball from going in the goal?'

He replied,

'Well, Bill Higgins, there were three balls comin' towards me and I grabbed the center ball.'

Judge Higgins ended with:

"Now, Governor John, when you get on your feet tonight, grab the center ball and you'll do ok."

One Saturday afternoon, the locker room boy answering the telephone heard a female voice say, "Is my husband there?"

The boy promptly answered, "No, ma'am."

"How can you say he isn't there before I even tell you who I am?"

"Don't make no difference, lady. There ain't never nobody's husband here."

DERM DUGGAN

THE BEST THING ABOUT CONFEDERATION

In May of 1952, I was asked to speak at a Lennox Furnace Co. convention at Woodbridge, Ontario.

When the chairman announced that the next speaker was to be a Newfoundlander, all heads started to look around trying to get a glimpse at this queer thing, a Newfoundlander. Some there did not know if it would be white, yellow or black.

(I remember being in Florida in 1948 and meeting an orchard owner and his two boys. The boys went home and told their mother about meeting some Newfoundlanders and they said, "Do you know what, Mom? Their skin is just like ours.)

To get back to the convention. I was in my Sunnyside Motel room that evening and about fifteen westerners came in to get a close up of a Newfoundlander. When they were satisfied that it was alive, they started asking me questions about confederation, the advantages and disadvantages, did I like it and what I had against it? Eventually, one fellow said, "Clouston, if there is one thing you like better than anything else about Confederation, would you tell us?"

"Sure", I said, "that eight hours of water between North Sydney and Port-aux-Basques."

HAULING SWOILES

Two "Greenpeacers" were listening to two oldtimers in St. Anthony discussing "swoilers." Of course, they knew that many Newfoundlanders referred to seals as swoiles.

Thinking to have some fun one of these Greenpeacers said to them, "How do you spell swoiles?"

One of the oldtimers replied quickly, "We don't spell 'em we hawls 'em."

THE ESSENCE OF CONTRARINESS

A Newfoundland couple had been married for many years. The wife was very patient because she had put up with a lot of contrariness from her husband. The incident which went a bit too far was when he came to breakfast one morning and she said,

Wife: What are ya goin' to 'ave fer yer brakfass?

Husband: Two h'eggs.

Wife: How do ya want 'em?

Husband: One boiled an' one fried.

She did as he requested and put the eggs on the table in front of him. When he scowled and frowned at the same time she said,

Wife: What's wrong now?

Husband: Ya boiled d' wrong one.

QUITE POSSIBLE

The following is taken from Francis Gay's, *The Friendship Book* which has something elevating for every day of the year and a little humour also.

A mischievous boy was asked by his mother: "How do you expect to get into heaven?"

He thought for a minute and then said, "Well, I'll just run in and out and keep slamming the door until they say 'For goodness sake, come in or stay out!' and then I'll go in."

PERCENTAGES

A Roman Catholic sister who was travelling all alone, found herself on an airliner seated directly in front of three protestant clergymen. She could overhear the conversation of the three which was mostly about the Roman Catholic denomination. Eventually one of the clergymen said, "I wished I lived in Canada. There are only 15% Catholics there. The next clergyman said he wished he lived in the United States, there are only 10% Catholics there. The third clergyman said, "You should live where I live, there's only 5% Catholics there."

Well the poor Catholic sister could take it no longer, so she turned around to them and said,

"WHY DON'T YOU ALL GO TO HELL THERE ARE NO CATHOLICS THERE!"

IT WAS A LESSON IN LISTENING

A teacher was observing a student who had not been paying much attention all through the mathematics lesson. It was getting near the end of the class when the teacher made an observation.

Teacher: "Well Bill, you're learning something."

Student, in surprise: "No, no sir, just listenin' to you."

A REVOLTIN' DEVELOPMENT TO BE SURE

Two fellows who belonged to King's Cove, B.B., were laid off from Buchans. After a day or two they decided to return home to King's Cove. Before they left Buchans they were half shot and by the time they arrived home in King's Cove they were ossified.

The next day neither one of them remembered going to the wake which was in progress when they arrived home. But one will always remember being at the wake because when he awoke the next morning he found himself in the same room with the carpse.

The carpse was horizontal in the coffin and our friend was horizontal on the couch parallel to the carpse. After boozing all the day previous you can imagine he wasn't feeling very good. He had a big head-plus.

After recovering from the shock of seeing the coffin, he eventually stood up and made the motion to leave the room, but before doing so, he went back, and looking down, he said to the carpse, "I don't know how you're feelin' but it got to be a heck of a sight better than the way I'm feelin'."

HE HAD TO SAY IT

I think it is true to say, that in most smaller communities of Newfoundland, the outports, everyone knows everyone else. It is in those areas that folklore humour evolves.

In 1955, Television first came to Newfoundland and the following story is true folklore humour.

In a certain community on the Southern Shore, television antennas started to stick up from one roof after another. A lady, who was always noted for her fancy hats came to mass one Sunday morning with an exceptionally tall feather sticking up from her hat. One gentleman who was noted for his humourous remarks about anything unusual, went over to this lady after mass and in a very lovely Irish vernacular said to her, "Well, Kit gurl, are ya gittin' a good reciption?"

SOCKED IN BUT NOT IN FOG

As a rule, when anyone says, "Al, did you hear about the Newfoundlander who—' usually I do just that, I cut him off in the middle of his sentence. Recently however, I did stop and the story was this.

A young Newfoundlander, fifteen years old, went to Toronto for ten days and his mother told him to put on clean socks everyday . . . the last day there, he couldn't get his boots on.

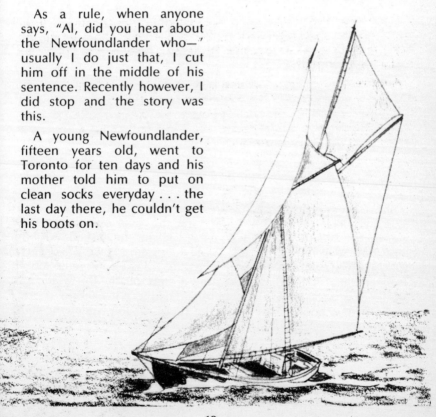

EDUCATION

Royal Readers were the standard of education in Newfoundland in years gone by. If you asked a fellow what education he had he could reply that he left school in the third book or the fifth book, all this meant Royal Reader numbers and each number was an advancement in school.

There has been many stories told about those readers and the most famous one in my opinion was the one about Mr. Mouland of the Newfoundland Disaster.

Some federal people came to Newfoundland after Confederation and made a survey to determine the level of education we had on the island. Visiting with Mr. Mouland they asked him how long he had spent in school. "Well," he said, "I went to school and on my startin' day they were readin' from a book tellin' about Tom and his dog. Someone threw a stick out in the water and Tom's dog went after it and before the dog got back to shore I was out of school." That meant he had probably spent the most of one morning in school.

Years ago when we had our street cars here in the city, a certain passenger was impatient with the slow pace so he approached the conductor with

TRIP TO BAY D'ESPOIR

About 1961, I made a visit to the Sou'West coast. Wishing to go to Bay D'Espoir, a friend and I travelled to Bay L'Argent, Fortune Bay, having in mind to join the Government coastal boat, the M.V. Bonavista, on Saturday afternoon. When we arrived there we were informed that the boat would not be there until six o'clock tomorrow morning. Well, it meant an ovenight stay in Bay L'Argent and where were we going to sleep, surely not the car. I said this out loud and a C.N. employee suggested Mrs. Pardy's for she had a boarding house. I went up to Mrs. Pardy's and this is the following conversation:

AL: "Mrs. Pardy, do you have a bed for my friend and me, until the Bonavista gets in tomorrow morning?"

MRS. PARDY: "Nar bed leaved now, zir. Dem all give up to salesmen and fellas like youse waitin' fer the Bonivess."

AL: "Well, what will we do now?"

MRS. PARDY: "Go up to Banfields and wait there and we'll send a taxi there to let yees know when the Bonivess gets in."

AL: "Nothing cookin'. That boat'll come in, the captain will drop his freight and away to go. He won't wait for us."

MY FRIEND: "Yer right, Al. Capt. Penney is abord dat Bonivess and he'll wait fer nobody. Last year down in St. Anthony he wouldn't wait half an hour fer me to finish a job. He said he wouldn't wait fer his own mother."

MRS. PARDY: "Too bad 'bout'n! His mudder 'ad to wait nine mont's on ee."

NEURALAGIE

Kevin Jardine is one of our best humourists who tells many funny stories which have their origin in St. John's. I met him on Water Street early this year and he told me about a character who lived in the west end of St. John's. His name was Mickey Brine. His Father Confessor was a resident Priest of St. Patrick's.

One morning, Mickey met the Priest and during the conversation he happened to say,

"FATHER WHAT'S DIS NEW DISEASE I WAS READIN ABOUT NEURALAGIE HOW DO YOU CATCH DAT?"

"WELL MICKEY, AS FAR AS I CAN TELL A FELLOW GETS IT BY NOT LOOKING AFTER HIMSELF. HES ALWAYS BOOZING UP A BIT, AND OUT IN THE COLD NEVER WORRYING WHERE NIGHT OVERTAKES HIM, AND PROBABLY LYING AROUND WHEN HES HAD TOO MUCH TO DRINK."

"OH, I SEE. WELL FATHER, I WAS ONLY ASKIN' BECAUSE I SEE BY THE PAPER, D' POPE HAS IT."

FALSE ALARMS

Over in the area of Conception Bay, a new fire engine had been bought by the local Municipal Council. Well, many people turned out to see the new engine and just about everyone admired it and many comments were made. One very comical fella came along and remarked, "It won't take many fires to pay fer she, will 'ee b'y."

One big problem was presenting itself to the council and that was what they were going to do with the old fire engine? It was decided to have a special meeting on this subject.

The meeting was held and many suggestions were made. On the council was one intelligent fellow from Upper Island Cove and everyone was waiting to hear his pronouncement. At last Uncle Charlie got to his feet and started in his usual slow but definitely Island Cove accent. "Mr. Chairman, I'd loike to make a proposal." The chairman said, "Uncle Charlie, will you putt'n in d'farm of a motion?" Uncle Charlie then replied, "If dat's what you wunts, I'll putt'n in d'farm of a motion. I moves, zir, we keeps 'er and uses 'er fer false alarms."

SOME COL' OL' MAN!

In November of 1977, I attended a wedding reception being held at Munday Pond Parish Hall. One of the guests was a gentleman from Grand Falls who had worked with the Price Co. for a good number of years.

He told me that it was normal to have low temperatures in the wintertime in Grand Falls. But one night the temperature had dropped extremely low. The next morning a number of the employees were discussing how cold it had been last night.

One fellow who was listening but had not commented, suddenly became excited and said, "Talk 'bout been col'! Youse fellas should a'been up 'long we upon d'ill lass night. Some col' up dere, ol' man! I scraped d'fross off d'windy dis marnin' and what do ya tink? Dere wuz d'wood-arse tryin' to get in d'barn.

Years ago when you brought your laundry to the Chinese laundry, you got a brown piece of paper as a receipt. Then when you returned to pick it up you produced the receipt, and you got your laundry spotlessly white. But a customer one day wondered what the Chinese characters meant and he said to his laundry man . . .

NERVOUSNESS IS FATAL

A young fellow had successfully completed his high school years in the small community three room school. He made a decision and announced to his mother that he would be leaving to study for the church. This pleased her very much and she was not long in letting others know the good news.

Since this meant his leaving and moving far away from them, many good wishers did what had always been done and it was traditional, a big going away party was held in the Parish Hall and several smaller parties as well. Our prospective candidate for the clergy was on his way.

News of his success in his studies kept filtering back to home and when he was ordained he returned for a holiday before taking up the work of a distant parish to which he had been assigned.

On his arrival home he met the resident minister and of course he thought it would be a good idea if the young minister would give the sermon on Sunday. No Way! How could he stand in the pulpit of the church where he had grown up, and give forth to all these people who had really helped rear him. He refused.

But his mother heard about it and of course her powers over her son prevailed and he consented for her sake.

Now the ancient little church had been rather neglected and had not had as much repairs done to it as should have been. When it came to the sermon on Sunday the resident minister made the announcement that there was no need to introduce the guest preacher, because the people knew the young fellow better than he did.

The young fellow stood in the front of the pulpit and without any preliminaries, he announced his text. "Behold, I Come". After that there was a dead silence. Again he said, "Behold, I Come". but that was as far as he could get. He could not overcome his nervousness, so he moved about a bit and then grabbing the old pulpit and breezing down on it hard, he said once more, "BEHOLD, I COME." Well the old pulpit gave way under his weight and he fell out into the front pews of the congregation and into the arms of the resident minister's wife. He got to his feet and excitedly said to her, "OH, My! I'm so sorry." She replied, "My son, don't worry one bit about it, you warned me three times".

THE ANTIQUE COLLECTOR

I have heard of many stories about antique collectors who came to Newfoundland shortly after Confederation. These individuals had a hey day for Newfoundland was a collector's paradise. There were houses full of very old handmade furniture and thousands of precious old china, crystal and glass.

The collectors knew the dollar value of these antiques. But the unfortunate fact is that many unscrupulous ones paid the owners only a fraction of the worth of each item.

Here, however, is a story of a very horrified antique collector. He was a clever fellow so he went into the barn to have a look around before going to the home of one of the older residents. To his delight he saw an old table that was worth at least $200.00. No doubt it had been layed aside in favour of one of our modern flashy looking chrome sets.

ALTERNATIVES!

A storekeeper in one of our outports found it was not too busy and decided to go into his residence, which was attached to his store, and have a shave.

He had washed his face and was all lathered up when someone came to the door. It was a little girl who had been sent to the store for some aspirin. He wiped off the lather and took care of the girl's requirement. He was all lathered up again when another knock was heard on the door. This time it was a feller who was goin' in d'woods, an' 'ad nar bit of backie. Now Cartny, ya can't go in d'woods widout backie. So our storekeeper again washed the lather from his face and got the old feller his baccie.

By this time he was rather "put out" but he was determined to get his shave so he announced he was goin' up stairs and this time nobody was to disturb him while he was up there.

He was not up there very long before his young son yelled out to say someone wanted him. "Who is it?", The son said, "Tis d'clergyman." The storekeeper yelled back, "If it's the Salvation H'army, 'ide the cash box; if it's the Roman Catholic priest, 'ide d'rum bottle; and if it's the H'anglican clergyman, tell yer mudder to sit on ee's lap till I comes down."

WHICH DENOMINATION

From a recent letter:
Hi Uncle Al,

"How ya gettin' on b'y. Good I hope. I'm doin' fine. I was just readin' *The Newfoundland Herald* when I came across your section. What a laugh! Well, I got a story for you. It's a true story about a guy right here from Summerford. Last summer, he went to Toronto for a holiday and he decided one day that he would have his dinner in a restaurant.

"When he came to pay the bill, he asked the cashier if she accepted traveller's cheques. (For anyone who doesn't know anything, these cheques come in 5, 10, 20, etc.) The cashier asked him what denomination and quickly without any hesitation, he said "Pentecost".

A LOW BLOW

A few weeks ago, I met an old friend from the bay. We have had many laughs through the years and it is customary for us to start laughing before many words are said. What a relationship! But this is true and with quite a few of my friends this is what happens.

However, my friend from the bay had a story. It is the type of story which you have to imagine you are there and viewing the situation from behind the curtain.

It appears that he went to visit his great uncle. He was not there very long before he felt the atmosphere rather tense. It was evident that uncle and aunt had surely had a disagreement. Words were few and not many of them at all.

When he had been there about half an hour, a knock came to the door, Aunt Mary answered it and a fellow selling encylopedias requested that he come in. Aunt Mary consented and the salesman came into the kitchen where we had been sitting. Right away he started his sales pitch which he followed for about five minutes. Suddenly he realized he would have to use a better approach and kept addressing Aunt Mary more than Uncle John. He made the following statement—"You should have this encyclopedia because when your grand-children come to visit and your nieces and nephews, they will ask questions and any answers you are not sure of you will find in this encyclopedia." Uncle John was not long in interrupting the saleman and made his own statement—"Young man, you're talking to the wrong woman now, cuz H'aunt Mary 'ere KNOWS H'EVERYTHING!"

LONELY AND MISERABLE

A friend of mine who is a widow told me that her husband had said to her on one occasion, "It is better to be lonely than miserable." Talking to a bachelor in the post office one day I related this to him. His reply was, "Do you know what I say—'tis better to be miserable alone."

UP SHE COMES

A niggardly farmer lost his wife and scrimped as much as he could on each phase of the funeral expenses, right down to the bitter end. Then he lingered in the graveyard after the mourners had gone, and asked the gravedigger, "How much do I owe you?"

"Ten dollars," said the gravedigger, who was just beginning to fill the grave.

"That's overmuch for such light sandy soil," said the farmer speculatively.

"Light sandy soil or rich loamy soil, ten dollars," said the gravedigger firmly, "OR UP SHE COMES."

The farmer hastily paid.

MORE BUMPER THUMPERS

The pedestrian had no idea which direction to go, so I ran over him.

The indirect cause of this accident was a little guy in a small car with a big mouth.

I saw the slow-moving, sad-faced gentleman as he bounced off the hood of my car.

I was thrown from my car as it left the road. I was later found in a ditch by some stray cows.

The accident happened when the right front door of a car came around the corner without giving a signal.

SOMETHING VERY OBVIOUS

Mrs. O'Toole: "Why are you giving me a dirty look, Mrs. Behan?"

Mrs. Behan: "I didn't give you a dirty look— you had it when I came in."

Two Newfoundlanders went to the mainland looking for jobs. They had had a number of other jobs but they were fussy fellows for they wanted weekends off. They were tired of trying and were fed up when they saw a sign by a garage . . .

BELIEVE IT OR NOT

A credible story which is really a Newfoundland "Believe It Or Not," is a story about a woman who died twice but on her first trip to the graveyard did not make the grave. I said credible because the man who told me had a man with him who vouched for the truth of the tale. It happened about 60 years ago.

Apparently, a woman died in one of the communities in the bay. The woman was waked in the church and the religious service was held on the day of the proposed burial. The coffin was placed on a horsedrawn wagon to the gate of the cemetery. Six pallbearers removed the coffin from the wagon and proceeded to carry it through the gate opening. Going through the opening the coffin was knocked heavily against one of the gate posts. Immediately a noise was heard coming from within the coffin. The cover was unfastened and to everyone's amazement the woman was alive.

She was taken back home by her husband and was soon doing her normal housekeeping. She lived on for 20 years and then died a second time.

As she was being carried through the gate on this occasion a pallbearer was heard to remark, "Now b'ys don't knock 'er agin' the gate this time."

TOO MUCH FITS NOWHERE

About three years ago I was in Toronto and visiting a very kind and gentle lady from Southern Ireland.

This lady is Teresa O'Driscoll who has a beautiful voice and was studying singing with my daughter, Carol Ann.

We were in her living room discussing a subject which involved a professor in university and when his name was mentioned she said in a beautiful Irish accent, "Al, some people are educated beyond their capacity," and then she added, "and too much fits nowhere."

AN EXPENSIVE FISHING EXPEDITION

As most people know, the Gander River has been famous for salmon fishing. For years now, guides have been available to fishing parties from other parts of Canada and the United States.

An American from New York arranged a fishing party. He had the guide meet him and his party from New York at Gander. They visited some of the choice fishing pools on the Gander River and a week later returned to Gander to get their flight back to New York.

The leader of the party had been only partially successful. He had caught only one salmon. As you can imagine, to come to Newfoundland for a week's fishing is quite expensive. The leader was not very backward in letting his listeners know his disappointment and how much it had all cost him.

While waiting for his flight, he went about the airport lobby announcing loudly in a very American accent: "ONE FISH, $2,000, THAT'S A LOT OF MONEY FOR ONE FISH, $2,000."

After an elderly Newfoundlander had heard this several times he got close to the American and said, "You're lucky, you didn't catch two."

First golfer: "Shall we play again next Saturday?"

Second golfer: "Well, I was going to get married on Saturday, but I can put it off."

GOOD FIGURING

A feller over 'ome promised his vote to the Liberal hopeful and then ten minutes later promised it to the P.C. candidate. His wife chastised him and he replied quite wisely:

"Did you notice how pleased each of the candidates were?"

"Yes."

"Well, I pleased dem both, an' on election day I'll please meself, an' den we will all be pleased t'gedder."

JOEY SMALLWOOD AND THE CORPSE

Just after our provincial elections in September of 1975, I was driving to Grand Falls for a speaking engagement. It was a Friday afternoon and university students were quite plentiful hitch-hiking home for the week end.

At the overpass, T.C.H. and Topsail Road, I picked up two students who were endeavouring to get to Greenspond, Bonavista Bay. When I said I was going to Grand Falls, it was right up their alley, because they would get one lift to Gambo. They were aboard for about an hour when one of them noticed a copy of my record "Spinnin' Yarns" on the seat. He said, "You are Al Clouston?" I confirmed this and he continued, "Well, we have a good story for you. In Greenspond, one morning just before the elections, and down on the wharf were six eldery men all in heated conversation about the elections. One gentleman was claiming it was a waste of money to have elections, saying the Liberals had twenty two years, why not give the P.C.'s a chance. Let them stay in power. Another claimed that in those twenty two years, the Liberals had not done much for Greenspond anyway, and P.C.'s are not going to do any better.

The whole conversation became very negative and soon everyone was condemmed. They were not very kind to Frank Moores and Ed Roberts was only one of Smallwood's babies anyway. Remarks about N.D.P. leader, Gerry Panting, were made. Then the conversation ended as follows:

"Who's dat feller, Pantin'? Anybody know ee?"

"No. I knows nuttin about ee. Ee's a new feller."

"How about Joey Smallwood?"

"JOEY SMALLWOOD? DAT COCKY FELLER! Everyting ee goes at ee wants to be d'ead of it. Most important feller dere."

"Yes, I know dat's true. Cuz I allow when Joey goes to a funeral, ee wants to be the corpse!"

OLD TIME FUNERALS

Not too long ago I heard a story about a wake. In this case, preparations got going early. The husband had been ill for several years and the doctor had visited regularly. This particular day the doctor found the patient in a much weakened condition and remarked to the wife that her husband would probably die today.

She got a big pot of soup going and about 10 o'clock at night made a visit upstairs. The first thing her poor husband had to say was,

"MARY DAT SOUP SMELLS GOOD, I'D LIKE A DROP"

"AH PAT B'Y CAN'T YA BE MORE CONSIDERATE? I'M SAVING THAT SOUP FER D' WAKE'

DEAR UNCLE AL

From Little Bay Islands, Green Bay:

Dear Uncle Al,

I enjoy reading your stories in *The Newfoundland Herald,* so I am sending you a couple for your column. This one, however, is a touchy incident as well as the man in the story is.

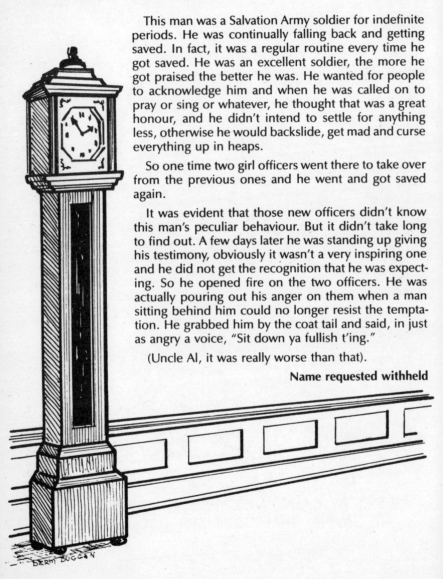

This man was a Salvation Army soldier for indefinite periods. He was continually falling back and getting saved. In fact, it was a regular routine every time he got saved. He was an excellent soldier, the more he got praised the better he was. He wanted for people to acknowledge him and when he was called on to pray or sing or whatever, he thought that was a great honour, and he didn't intend to settle for anything less, otherwise he would backslide, get mad and curse everything up in heaps.

So one time two girl officers went there to take over from the previous ones and he went and got saved again.

It was evident that those new officers didn't know this man's peculiar behaviour. But it didn't take long to find out. A few days later he was standing up giving his testimony, obviously it wasn't a very inspiring one and he did not get the recognition that he was expecting. So he opened fire on the two officers. He was actually pouring out his anger on them when a man sitting behind him could no longer resist the temptation. He grabbed him by the coat tail and said, in just as angry a voice, "Sit down ya fullish t'ing."

(Uncle Al, it was really worse than that).

Name requested withheld

THE WORRIED WIFE

One evening in 1975, I was asked to address the gathering at a dinner being held by the Odd Fellows Society.

The dinner was over and an old gentleman came up to me and said, "Mr. Clusson, I lived in the houtports too one toime, an' dere wuz a woman dere who wuz wunerful seeck. She wuz martally hill. The doctor only give 'er six months. The toime wuz mose up and one day she looked up from her bid an' said:

"'ARRY I KNOWS YOU IDDN'T TOO HOLD TO GIT MARRIED AGIN, I'D BE AT THE SAME TING IF I WUZ YOUR HAGE, BUT DERES ONE TING I GOT TO H'ASK YA."

"WHAT'S DAT MAID?"

"DAT YER NEW WOMAN WON'T WEAR MY CLOTHES."

"MY FLOSSY! NO WORRY 'BOUT DAT MAID, NO CONCARN AT ALL. YOUR CLOTHES TWICE TOO BIG FER BESSIE."

HERE'S ANOTHER WATERLOO STOVE STORY

Uncle Ank, he seemed to draw trouble like a magnet—in fact—trouble was his middle name—he always seemed to be into a scrape.

Whatever he went at usually ended up in disaster for him, even things of the most simplicity. Take for instance the time old Jake's wharf fell down at high tide. Well you see Uncle had to be on that wharf that particular time now didn't he!

And take for instance the time he chopped the head off the chicken and threw it down in front of a dog that had been eating fish for half the year. And the dog grabbed the hen and crawled under the house with it, and ate it feathers and all. Wouldn't blame it one bit, not 'every other day it got a feed of chicken.

But this time I am writing about concerns and again the old Waterloo Stove. Uncle had got the old stove from someone across the harbour and brought it home and left it in the skiff off on the collar. When the tide rose he got his punt to carry it to the beach near his house for easy transportation, rather than take it to the stage head and then having to hawl it up over the wharf.

So himself and the young feller (a boy he had raised up and always called the "young feller"—as most young boys were these times rather than their name if they happened to be the youngest) they rowed into the beach with the stove on board—threw out the grapnel and the punt swung broadside to the lops rolling shoreward.

Then they lifted out the Waterloo Stove and placed it on the beach, and then Uncle told the young feller to steady the boat while he himself lifted out the oven. Standing on the gangboards he picked up the oven and stood up to step ashore.

Well no one really knows what happened next but the young feller's mind must be elsewhere as the boat rolled over and away goes Uncle arse over kettle right overboard and a geyser of water shot skyward.

Talk about a slouse, oh boy, he was not so lucky as Peter as he was holding a Waterloo oven and he hit rock bottom. A couple men who were mending some linnet on the bawn nearby saw it all—a flurry of foam and thrashing arms and legs and a partly submerged oven.

As Uncle broke water he was in a state of shock—to say the least and after crawling ashore he just stood there, his mouth working and no sound coming forth as he looked around for the young feller.

Fearing apoplexy the two fishermen came to his aid—sent him home—fished out the oven and took the oven to his house on a hand barrow. The young feller was long gone. He had made his exist as Uncle's two Excel rubbers disappeared over the side, and the only thing stood good for him was that if Uncle thought t'was accidental.

That was not Uncle's only dousings in sea water. He could have learned to scuba dive that way. But he never died by drowning, he lived to be 88 years old and God rest him.

IS GOD DEAD?

Some years ago, an article appeared in a Canadian magazine and was circulated through the newspapers. Many comments were made on the subject and written opinions pro and con appeared in the media. The caption of the article was "Is God Dead?"

Some time afterwards, a mainland salesman had to remain at a fairly remote settlement in Newfoundland over the weekend. He went to church on Sunday morning and the clergyman preached on this subject, "Is God Dead?"

After church, the salesman introduced himself to various age groups who stood outside the church after the service was over.

Finally, he went and introduced himself to the oldest group. He was very pleasant and explained his business for being there and said how much he had enjoyed attending the service. Before he left them, he turned to one of the old gentlemen and the following took place:

"NOW YOU HEARD THAT SERMON THIS MORNING?"

"YIS ZIR"

"WELL, WOULD YOU BELIEVE THAT GOD IS DEAD?"

"NEVER KNOWED EH WUZ SICK, OL' MAN!"

CHILDREN SAY THE DARNEDEST THINGS

A superintendent of a Sunday school had to substitute one Sunday morning for a teacher who was absent. He kept asking questions of the children and eventually asked:

"Where does God live?"

"In the bathroom in our house."

In surprise the superintendent asked, "Why do you say that Jim?"

"Cuz every morning in our house, Dad comes and bangs on the bathroom door and shouts, 'GOOD LORD! ARE YOU STILL IN THERE,?'"

HARD TO PLEASE

A couple of co-workers were coming off shift and one said, "Come on, let's go and have a beer". His friend replied, "No b'y, I got to go home and explain". "Explain What?" "I don't know. I have to wait until I go home".

The same fellow had a wife who was difficult to please and it did not matter what he did he should have done it the other way.

When his birthday came around she went shopping and bought him two ties. When he was dressing he saw the package and opened it. He thought he might please his wife by wearing one of the ties right away that morning. When he came to breakfast she looked across the table at him and remarked, "Ah! You didn't like the other one, did ya".

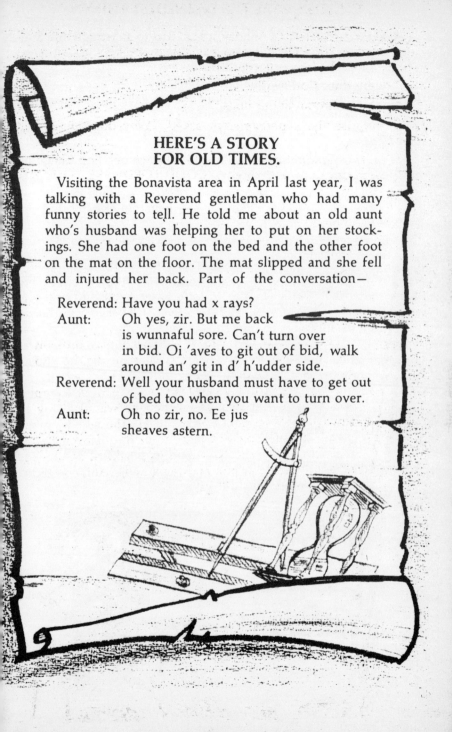

HERE'S A STORY
FOR OLD TIMES.

Visiting the Bonavista area in April last year, I was talking with a Reverend gentleman who had many funny stories to tell. He told me about an old aunt who's husband was helping her to put on her stockings. She had one foot on the bed and the other foot on the mat on the floor. The mat slipped and she fell and injured her back. Part of the conversation—

Reverend: Have you had x rays?

Aunt: Oh yes, zir. But me back
is wunnaful sore. Can't turn over
in bid. Oi 'aves to git out of bid, walk
around an' git in d' h'udder side.

Reverend: Well your husband must have to get out
of bed too when you want to turn over.

Aunt: Oh no zir, no. Ee jus
sheaves astern.

THE OLD LADY AND THE PILLS

Bob MacLeod has been one of Newfoundland's greatest and most popular entertainers for approximately fifty years. He is a master of the piano and organ and very few could compare when it came to interpreting the way Newfoundland songs are to be sung. He had a wealth of funny Newfoundland stories and on stage used those stories and his piano to entertain his audience.

The following is a story the circumstances of which took place in the early forties.

The old call letters of the radio station which was owned by the Newfoundland Government was VONF. This was before Confederation. Bob worked at that radio station and two of his co-workers were fellows from Carbonear, Conception Bay. One of them told him this story and the other confirmed it.

An old lady was on the platform of the railway station at Carbonear and she said to the conductor, "Let me know when we gets to Brigus Junction, wunt ya?" He assured her he would. But he forgot all about the old lady until the train was five miles beyond Brigus Junction. Well, he stopped the train and backed it up to Brigus Junction. (And for the benefit of mainland readers, we did just that when we owned the railway in Newfoundland. It was for our convenience.)

Anyway, the conductor looked for the old lady and then this conversation ensued:

CONDUCTOR: "I'm sorry to delay you this marnin' but we're back to Brigus Junction agin now, you kin git out."

LADY: "Oh! I don't want to git out."

CONDUCTOR: "No! How come?"

LADY: "Well, me zon, I wuz down to Carbonear dis marnin' to see doctah, an' ee gimme some pills, an' ee said to take one den and when I gits to Brigus Junction to take annudder one."

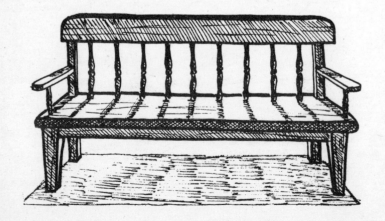

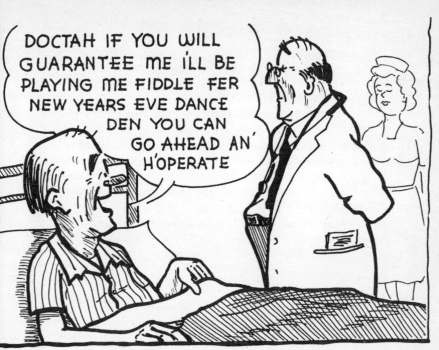

43

THE PENGUIN STORY

A Torontonian was on his way to the zoo with two hundred penguins in his truck. He experienced some mechanical trouble and had pulled onto the shoulder of the highway and was there for a considerable time. A Newfoundlander was going by in his truck and noticed the Torontonian. He stopped and got out of his truck and asked him. "What's d'trouble old cock?" Reply. "I'm taking two hundred penguins to the zoo and my truck has broken down". The Newfoundlander said, "B'y, my truck is as big as yours, lets put 'em in my truck. I'll take them to the zoo". The Torontonian was very pleased, transferred the penguins and gave the Newfoundlander $200.00 to take them to the zoo.

Fine. About ten o'clock that night the Torontonian was walking down Yonge Street and saw the Newfoundlander coming up the street with the two hundred penguins following him.

Torontonian: Hey Buddy, I told you to take those penguins to the zoo.

Newfoundlander: I took them to the zoo. You gave me $200.00 and I have some left over, so now I'm taking them to the movies.

✓TURNIPS ARE KEPT IN THE CELLAR

The Magistrate had held court in the school house. The trial of Joe was over. Joe had been proven guilty beyond doubt. He had stolen on three occassions from the general store. The plaintiff was amazed when the Magistrate had ruled a suspended sentence.

Magistrate: You can't get blood from a turnip.

Plaintiff: No. But you can put it in the cellar for thirty days.

THE SUPER AND THE MAN FROM ISLAND COVE

Long before The Dominion Wabana Mining Co. over in Bell Island shut down, and when everything as we would say was going "full tilt", many of the miners were fellows from various places in Conception Bay. I think all will admit that the wittiest fellows were from Island Cove.

One of these was a chap who had been warned on several occasions that his actions were endangering the lives of others. These warnings were not having the desired result and one day when he arrived back to the surface, the super called him into his office and the following conversation took place:

45

PENGUINS ENJOY THE ZOO

Here we are laughing at ourselves again.

This story takes place in Ontario. A driver of a transport truck suddenly found his vehicle inoperable. For an hour or more he tried to signal other drivers that he was in trouble. At last a transport truck of the same size as his stopped. The driver was a Newfoundlander.

When he walked up to the Ontario driver he said, "What's d'matter wid you old cock?"

The reply was, "Well my truck has broken down and I got a real problem. On board are 200 penguins which I am taking to the zoo in Toronto, and I can't leave them here on the highway and go looking for help."

The Newfoundlander solved the problem by suggesting, "Look 'ere, my truck is as big as yours; let's put 'em all in my truck and I'll take 'em to d'zoo fer yez."

So it was agreed. They transferred the penguins from one truck to the other. Then the Ontario chap took out a roll of paper money and gave the Newfoundlander $250 to take the penguins to the zoo.

About 10 o'clock that night the Ontario chap saw the Newfoundlander coming up Yonge Street with the 200 penguins following him. In his amazement he went up to the Newfoundlander and said, "Look here, I gave you $250 to take these penguins to the zoo!"

The Newfoundlander replied, "Dat's right b'y. Yes, and I had some change left over. They enjoyed the zoo so now I'm takin' 'em to the movies."

THE HUMOR OF EVERY DAY

I like the remark that makes this story click.

At a missonary meeting some years ago, one of the speakers said in his address that there were still some 3,000 cannibals in the South Sea Islands. He also remarked that four missionaries were to be sent to them.

An old farmer leaned across and whispered to his neighbour, "Four won't go far among three thousand."

THE IMPORTANT THING IS TO EAT

Some years ago my paper boy Tom, came to be paid one Saturday morning. With him was his young brother. I said to Tom, "Any more home like him?" "Yes sir four." "That makes six of you," I said. Then the five year old spoke up with "Dere's eight of us sir, dere's me fauder and mudder."

Next I said, "Who does all the cooking?" The five year old said "Oi gets me own breakfast." "Do you cook it or pour it out of a carton?"

The five year old, "Oi eats it."

VIGILANTE JUSTICE

Most Newfoundlanders are familiar with the fact that up until recent years, the fuel for heat and cooking throughout most of our island, was wood. We also know that our people were most diligent in having a one or two year supply always on hand. Each household had a standing stock of sticks which were left to dry near the residence.

Much labour went into the procuring of the wood supply. Members of each family went in country to their favourite tree stand in the winter, cut their wood and hauled loads of it to home over frozen lakes and through well worn paths to the community where they lived.

In a certain outport an old fellow started losing some of his wood from the woodpile. He put up with it for a long while until it started to get serious. He was losing quite a lot of wood, so find the culprit he must. So one day he bored some holes in some of the sticks of wood, filled them with gun powder and plugged them up.

A few days later everyone knew who the thief was. Use your own imagnation. People in those days sometimes administered their own justice when necessary. Lets call it "Vigilante Justice."

SAUCEY TEETH

Ted Skakum is a denturist who practices his profession on the south west coast of Newfoundland.

Ted told me about a lady for whom he had made a set of false teeth. When she came to have them fitted she happened to bring along her husband. He asked the man to wait in another room while he did the fitting. At the completion of his work Ted asked the husband to come and see if he approved.

Ted: What do you think of these teeth?

The husband stood in front of his wife and as she stretched her mouth from one side to the other he said: "Do dis,—Now do dis," then he exclaimed. "De're alright as long as de're not as saucy as d'last set she had.

BROWN TOAST

A salesman told me about going into a small restaurant with two of his friends and ordered their breakfast.

The ordering was completed and the waitress was walking away when he said, "Oh yes, and I'll have brown toast!" The waitress came back to their table and said, "Look 'ere, we puts 'en in da toaster an' eh toast 'en. An' dat's da way you'll git en".

PRIEST AND BEER BOTTLES

Visiting Bonavista for a few days in October 1979, my wife and I were entertained by a visitor who came one evening to the house where we were staying. He told us stories about happenings of thirty or forty years ago, which took place where he lived. The following is such a story.

The Roman Catholic priest of that area had to attend a meeting in St. John's for four or five days. The regular caretaker was indisposed and the priest employed a nineteen year old young fellow to see to things while he was away.

On the third day of the priest's absence, the young chap wandered down to the basement of the rectory and noticed, amongst other things, about twenty cases of empties. The next day he thought he would examine the contents of the cases. During this operation the priest returned unexpectedly and surprised the young caretaker.

TRUTHFUL . . . BUT SOME STUNNED

If we look up the word 'physic' in the dictionary we will find one meaning as relating to a medicine such as taking some laxative. When any medicine was taken for the express purpose as a laxative it was referred to as a physic.

Just before Christmas I was visiting some friends in Bloomfield, Bonavista Bay, and we were discussing courses offered by the Memorial College before it became a full-fledged university. Mr. Parsons told me that he had chosen physics as one of his subjects and it was a new subject to him.

When Professor Hatcher came to the lecture room to hold the first class, he asked Mr. Parsons, "What do you know about physics?"

Claude replied, "The only thing I know about physics, sir, is a dose of salts or senna tea."

HEAVEN

The Sunday School of five year olds had been listening attentively to stories about heaven and what a beautiful place it was. The teacher was careful to explain that only good children would be allowed to live in heaven.

Then she enthusiastically asked the question, "Now, who would like to go to heaven?" All the children stood up except one. "Why don't you want to go to heaven, Cynthia?" "Because Mommie said I was to come straight home after Sunday School."

EULOGY AND CORPSE DIDN'T MATCH

In a Catholic community in Newfoundland the priest was giving a eulogy to a deceased husband during the funeral mass. He kept making complimentary remarks about the man in the coffin. His praise for the deceased was so high that the widow was very doubtful whether or not it was about her dead husband that the priest was making his remarks. The man she knew and lived with was not that gentle and kind. So when the priest was finished the eulogy and sat down, she poked her daughter with her elbow and said.

"GO UP DERE AND SEE IF DATS YER FAUDER IN THE COFFIN"

OVERHEARD

An old lady was reading from the newspaper. It was about something a person had done that shocked the community. She put the paper down and said "Well, it takes all kinds to make a world, but I'm glad I'm not one of them".

DOGS CAN'T TAKE IT, BUT DOCTORS CAN

Dr. Walter Templeman spent many years serving the residents of Belt Island, Conception Bay. Sometimes people would call at night and he could tell pretty well whether they really needed a doctor or not. But he would always make sure and he would make the call.

Once when he had been out all evening making calls in a raging snow storm, he received one of these calls from a client who lived about two miles away. He felt it was one of those unnecessary calls. The husband assured him that his wife was truly sick this time. He consented but he told the man to come to meet him. "What?" the man said, "tackle up the horse and go out on a night like this. Doc, b'y, you wouldn't put a dog out on a night like this."

HOLY WIT

The following story comes from Scotland, taken from a book titled *Holy Wit*.

One New Year Sunday a Helmsdale Minister rebuked his church officer, not only for arriving late for evening service, but also for being the worse for drink, and for falling asleep during the sermon. The man excused himself by saying that he had been up the Strath that afternoon, and then added, "You know what it is like at New Year."

"I know perfectly well," replied the minister. "I was up the Strath myself this afternoon visiting, and I am not in the state you are in."

"No," agreed the beadle, "but you are not as popular as I am."

WHAT A BARBER CAN MANAGE

A Newfoundlander was in a Toronto barber shop. When he was asked if there was any special way he wished to have it cut, he replied,

SICK TIRED AND NOT TOO WELL

The Gerald S. Doyle News Bulletin was a great service to the Newfoundland people, especially the outport people. It broadcast many messages of all kinds. A sample was the hospital report which gave people back home a report on how their relatives were making out in hospital, a report on their progress and when they expected to be discharged from the hospital. The patients also enjoyed hearing about themselves.

One particular patient who had been in hospital for ten days and did not hear his name mentioned on the radio decided that tomorrow he would do something about it.

He was up early the next morning and, walking in the corridor, he met Dr. Pat Whelan and said, "Pardon me now zir but is youse a doctah?"

Pat said yes he was and our patient continued, "Well doctah my name is Billy Jones. Glad to talk wid ya zir. Good-bye now."

That night Pat Whalen was listening to the Doyle message news and he heard a special from Billy Jones to his family, "Saw doctor today. Feelin' fine."

SHE WAS POISONED

Two fellows were discussing marriage and the conversation eventually went like this.

First fellow: "Well, how many times were you married?"

Second fellow: "Three times b'y."

First fellow: "What? Three times. Are any of them living?"

Second fellow: "No b'y. All dead."

First fellow: "What happened to your first wife?"

Second fellow: "She died of mushroom poisoning."

First fellow: "And your second wife?"

Second fellow: "Same thing b'y, mushroom poisoning."

First fellow: "And what happened to your third wife?"

Second fellow: "She died of a heavy blow to the head."

First fellow: "What happened?"

Second fellow: "She wouldn't eat her mushrooms."

YOGA THE CORE

A notorious drunkard-about-town was persuaded to take up yoga to pull himself together. After 10 months of torturing long-unused muscles, he became quite proficient at it, too.

"His yoga helped him?" his wife was asked.

"In one way," she answered. "Now he can get drunk standing on his head too."

WHAT WAS MOST NEEDED

About fifty years ago, a minister over _ _ _ _ had persuaded his congregation to redecorate the interior of the church and at a church meeting he was complimenting the parishioners on a job well done. He then pointed out that just one thing more was needed to make the sanctuary a place of real beauty. He said he had spoken to the Board of Deacons about a new chandelier, and wondered what the decision would be. The chairman of the board came slowly to his feet and reported as follows:

"I don't think the board will recommend that, Reverend, and for three reasons. In the first place none of us could spell it. In the second place if we got one, there's no one could play it. And in the third place what this church really needs is better light."

WHAT DID OLD MACDONALD HAVE?

Three men answered a newspaper advertisement for a job, a Quebecer, a Torontonian and a Newfoundlander. Each one was interviewed separately and had to meet certain qualifications. They were interviewed in this order—the Quebecer, the Torontonian and the Newfoundlander.

However, there was one question which each one was asked and if he did not answer correctly he was eliminated.

They were to fill in the last word in this line: "Old MacDonald had a ——." The Quebecer's answer was house and the Torontonian's answer was barn. Of course they were both eliminated.

When the interviewer came to the Newfoundlander he said, "Well, all Newfoundlanders are smart fellas, surely you can answer this question correctly. Old MacDonald had a ——?"

Examiner: "Right on! Now spell it."

Newfoundlander: "Horse."

Examiner: "Right on! Now spell it."

Newfoundlander: "E.I.E.I.O."

LOBSTERS BY D'EACH

My friend Jimmy Martin, who does a great deal of travelling in Newfoundland, told me about wanting to buy some lobsters. He went down to the beach where some lobsters had just been landed. A young fellow had about two hundred in his crate.

JESUS OR SANTA CLAUS?

A little girl was asked who she liked best, Jesus or Santa Claus.
She said, "Santa Claus."
"Why?"
"Because, for Santa Claus, you only have t be good for a week, but for sus, you have to be good all the year round."

KEEP AN EYE ON YOUR GIRL FRIEND

When talking about the old Newfoundland Railway, the station at Goobies was referred to often by ardent anglers. Today it is referred to more often as the point at which you depart from the Trans Canada Highway and proceed down the highway to the Burin Peninsula.

Two years ago I arrived at Goobie's at 2:00 P.M. I was on my way to Grand Bank and stopped for a lunch at the Irving Service Station. After telling a couple of stories one of the ladies on the staff at the restaurant told me this story.

She said that last night a fellow stopped his car at the gas pump, told the attendant to fill the tank and then he proceeded to the washroom. He then came from the washroom, paid for the gas, got aboard his car and drove off.

Two hours later when he arrived in town and stopped at his mother's home, he opened the rear door of the car and told his girl friend to wake up, they were in St. John's. But, no girl friend was there. What a surprise. What happened?

At Goobies when he had gone to the washroom she was in the back of the car asleep. But she woke up, and also went to the washroom. He did not know this and proceeded on his way without her.

When he realized what had happened he drove right back to Goobie's, 100 miles. When he arrived back there, he was told she had left an hour before on the C.N. bus.

A MATTER OF INSURANCE

An old lady was very disturbed about losing her diamond ring. She told all her family about it and then suddenly remembered it was insured. She contacted the insurance agent and told him the circumstances under which she had lost it. It was quite apparent to him that the ring was only mislaid but after about three months the company was under considerable pressure and paid her the $1,200.00.

The company asked her to keep an eye out for the ring and advise them. Another three months went by and the insurance agent came around to see her. He asked her if she had found the diamond ring and she replied, "Oh my yes, I found the ring and I did not think it was right for me to keep the ring and the money, so I sent the $1,200.00 to the Red Cross."

A SEEK HOARSE, BUT HE DIED

I visited Renews on the Southern Shore to entertain at a Kinsmen meeting. After the meeting, a man came along and told me this story.

"Mr. Clusson, a man up d'shore had a hoarse an' he was seek." He met his friend and he said:

He went home and gave 'um da turpentine an' den he met his friend again.

"How did ya yet on wid d'hoarse? Did ya give 'um d'turpentine?"

"Yes I did."

"What happened?"

59

ELEPHANTS ARE NOT FOR TORONTO

A Newfoundlander was standing on the corner of College Street and Yonge for a whole week. He kept on clicking his fingers and saying "Keep out! Keep out! Don't come in here."

A Torontonian who had been hearing this each day as he passed became quite curious and asked the Newfoundlander what was he up to and the reply was "Keeping the elephants out of Toronto."

The Torontonian reacted quickly and said loudly, "MY DEAR MAN THERE IS NOT AN ELEPHANT WITHIN A THOUSAND MILES OF TORONTO."

So the Newfoundlander quietly said,

GARBAGE!

A lady had gotten an early start on her preparation for an evening out.

Her hair was up in curlers which were sticking off from her head in all directions. The first stage of a facial had been just completed, which consisted of having her face covered with a grayish, muddy looking material.

At this point she heard the approach of the garbage truck. She donned her house coat and in the same motion hurried down over the flight of steps to the side walk, and announced,

THE CANDLE HELPED

A young Roman Catholic couple were quite disappointed that after five years of married life, no offspring was in sight. On one occassion when their priest visited, they discussed the subject with him. He suggested that they put up a light as a remedy for the situation. They advised him that they had done so on several occassions but without success.

On the priest's next visit he said that he had been chosen to make a visit to Rome and while there he would light a candle in Rome for them and probably that would start things happening.

On his return to Newfoundland he was transferred to another parish and did not see the childless couple for about four years. When he did visit them, however, he discovered that they now had five children, two sets of twins and one single. He remarked to the wife "My, my, the candle in Rome worked? Where is your husband?" The reply, "Gone to Rome to blow out that Candle."

ONE ON THE MAINLANDERS

A visiting clergyman from the mainland told the following story at a meeting in the parish hall. I liked him for it because at last I had met a mainlander who was laughing at himself—the mainlander—something we Newfoundlanders do best of all.

He told the story about a certain section of Toronto where living was pretty rough. The owner of the beer parlour couldn't find a bouncer strong enough to keep order in the establishment. He resorted to getting a gorilla and trained him to remove the rowdies out onto the sidewalk. He chained the gorilla to a strong pillar in the corner and when a fight broke out he would let the gorilla go and peace was restored in short order.

One night a Newfoundlander came to the beer parlour and got involved in a fight. In about five minutes he knocked out four or five patrons. The gorilla was set loose and the Newfoundlander and the gorilla went through the door struggling, door shut. In about two minutes the door opened and the Newfoundlander came back in, shut the door, dusted himself off and then said loudly:

"DAT'S D'TROUBLE WIT' DEM MAINLANDERS. YA PUTS A FUR COAT ON 'EM AN' DEY T'INKS DEY OWNS D'WORLD."

PROPER TING!

You don't have to live in Newfoundland very long before you start to learn some of our local expressions, and they belong solely to Newfoundland.

I would like to tell about one expression which we use all over the Island and it is used when you are in total agreement with what you have been told or something which you happen to see and like, and you burst out with PROPER TING! It is a very positive affirmation of agreement and most times if you are sitting near a table, you bang the table with your fist as you proclaim PROPER TING!

In 1973 Peter Gzowski came to Newfoundland when he was host of the radio show "This Country in the Morning". Mrs. Marg Kearney was kind to me and asked me to come and be interviewed by Peter and I agreed.

At one point in the interview Peter said, "Al, in nearly every area of Canada where I visit, the people have a very commonly used expression. Does Newfoundland have one?" I replied, "Yes, we do." "What is it?" I said, "PROPER TING." Peter repeated right after me, "PROPER THING." "NO, NO," I said, "there is no H in it. You say TING." "Well," he said "What does it mean?" I replied, "You are seconding the motion. Look, someone says 'let's have a game of cards' and right away you confirm the idea with PROPER TING! (Banging your fist down of course.) Or he suggests 'let's go fishin'', PROPER TING! and sometimes a fella gets a poke in the face and that's the PROPER TING, too. As long as you agree with it, it is the PROPER TING."

Then Peter said, "Do you have a good story on PROPER TING?" I replied, "Yes, I was going up Water Street one morning and immediately ahead of me was a real Englishman who was a very good friend of mine. I got up behind him and said, "Mauzie day, isn't it, Huncle?" He turned around and laughingly said in a very rounded O English accent, "Oh, Alwyn, I have a good story for you. Down

COSTLY CONFESSION

A story on confession is told about the Rev. Father Coady in Tor's Cove.

A lady came to confession and the way she concluded the Rev. Father felt that she was not telling all, so he said, "Come on, come on, haven't got time to be wastin'."

WINNING BY SUGGESTION

In the early days of "snipe" sailing in the 1940's at Long Pond, Manuels, I was a member of the club.

When it was too windy to sail, it was normal for members to sit around and chat. One of our ardent members was Dr. E. F. Moores. We called him Dinty. Whenever Dinty decided he wanted to win a race, he won it. He was a great favourite at the club. There were times when Dinty came first in a race but disqualified himself for some breach of the rules. This was done just to encourage some young member of the club who had come in second.

One Wednesday half holiday afternoon, Dinty was telling of a few humourous instances in his life. This particular afternoon he told us one morning he went to his surgery and occupying the waiting room were four young ladies whom he knew were not regular patients of his. Not long before this occurred, he had decided not to increase his practice by adding new patients.

So Dinty went into his surgery, picked up a magazine and read for about ten minutes. He then looked at his watch and announced, "Ladies, I don't think that doctor is coming this morning. I wouldn't wait for him if I were you. I'm not going to wait." He then left his office and the four ladies did likewise. He boarded his car, drove around the block a few times and returned to his office.

GRADE SEVEN

It was the period in the school schedule when grade seven had a lesson on religion. The teacher was doing the best he could on the subject of eternity. Getting near the end of the period and wanting to see how well he had done, he asked the students what their understanding of eternity was. One girl of 12 spoke up and said, "Well sir, last Christmas Dad bought a new chesterfield and when Mom came from the H.F.C. last week, she said that the way she was paying it off, it would take 'til eternity."

Once when an Evangelist was addressing an open air meeting, an atheist kept throwing questions at the preacher. He did a good job at giving the answers. Eventually the atheist thought he would stump the reverend for sure . . .

WHIZGIGGIN

A university student had asked me to give him a few of the words or sayings of old Newfoundland which are little used today. I gave him what I had, but I kept on trying to obtain a few more for him.

One day on Water Street, I met Val Goodyear. I asked Val about it and he asked me if I had ever heard of Whizgiggin. I said "no", so then he said "Many times I got the back of my grand-father's hand for whizgiggin'". If you can imagine the following scene, you will learn what whizgiggin' is.

Here are four or five adults sitting in an outport kitchen, having what they consider a sensible discussion on one or two topics of the day, mostly about politics, cartny. Then, over in the corner are two or three children giggling and laughing about really nothing.

It is disturbing to the adults so the grand-father leans over the back of his chair at the same time reaching towards the children and making a rather mild swipe at them, says, "STOP YER WHIZGIGGIN'."

A MURDER

A story which my father told me was about an ardent trout fisherman who would use nothing but flies. He did not believe in using bait. With bait a trout did not have a sporting chance.

On Duckworth Street in old St. John's, a man had died and his neighbour was this particular fisherman. He was asked, "Mr. Spearns are you going to Dan's funeral?" "No, he's a murderer". "How do you make that out?" "HE CAUGHT TROUT WITH A WORM".

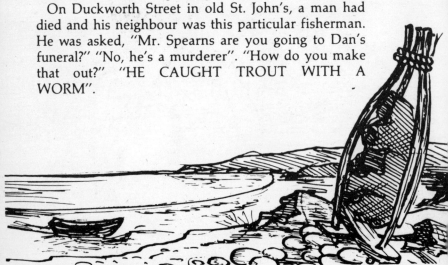

QUESTIONABLE CONCLUSION

A true man of the cloth is one who has compassion for a fellow traveller under any conditions. The following story surely puts this pastor in a special category.

A man who had evidently had one too many got aboard the bus and was finding it heavy weather keeping his feet under him. A Minister aboard the bus watched the man for a few minutes and then stood up and motioned to the poor fellow to sit. When seated the fellow looked up at the Minister and in a thick accent said, "Thank you padre. You're the only one aboard this bus who knows what it is like to be drunk."

GET THIS FOR GRATITUDE

A very happy rescuer was being commended by people standing around the shore of the pond where he had just saved a little boy from drowning. Suddenly the attention of everyone was distracted by a very large and loud woman who was making her way towards the rescuer with her apron and hair flying in the wind.

Woman: Are you d'man who saved me b'y?

Rescuer: Yes mam, I am.

Woman: Well den, where's eh's cap?

SICK, TIRED AND NOT TOO WELL

I'll begin by telling you a short story. In Riverhead, St. Mary's, I had a beautiful old friend. She was the wife of my guide Peter Lee. Well Mrs. Marie had arthritis for many years, but she knew if she didn't fight it she would become a victim and be a cripple—so fight it she did. Anyway, one leg persisted in losing much of its circulation and became permanently cool. She used to say that if she couldn't see it she did not know where it was—no feeling in it.

Her language was always very descriptive with a little humour thrown in. She was one of the old old school and did not believe that women smoked. On one occasion it was proven to her without doubt that a certain woman had been smoking while in bed and had caught the house on fire. When it eventually got through to Mrs. Lee that it was true she burst forth with:

"Blessed Virgin! 'Tis a pity almighty God didn't put her mouth back of her ear."

GUILTY ONE WAY OR THE OTHER

The following humorous incident did take place but not in Newfoundland.

In June I attended the "Citizen of Year" Dinner at the Newfoundland Hotel. The appointing of this honourable individual is always sponsored by the J.C.'s. This year their special speaker for the day was the President of the Bar Association of Canada.

He told a story about a court case which took place in Western Canada. It is so similar to a Ted Russell story that it is worth recording.

A man stole a horse. The individual from whom the horse was stolen was rather a detestable character which nobody cared much about. The trial was held before a Jury and the Judge told them there was no doubt about the verdict they should bring in.

The Jury was only out an hour when they returned.

Judge: Have you reached a verdict?

Foreman: Yes, your honour. Not guilty, but the accused must return the horse.

Well the Judge was furious and he sent the Jury back out. In a very short time the Jury returned again.

Judge: Have you reached a verdict?

Foreman: Yes your honour. Guilty, but the accused can keep the horse.

70

THE QUESTION OF AGE

A census taker was proceeding this morning with his routine work, just the same as he had done yesterday.

He came upon a spinster who refused to answer the question pertaining to age. After all other questions had been dealt with he returned to the question of age but received the same stony resistance. Eventually she said,

BROTHERLY LOVE.

Two brothers from the Northern Peninsula went to Corner Brook and bought a pretty dilapidated car for about three hundred dollars. They managed to get it home and then the next piece of business was for each brother to get his drivers licence.

An appointment was made with the local R.C.M.P. detachment and only one brother turned up for his test. The R.C.M.P. officer got in and told the boy to proceed down the road. After about a quarter of a mile he realized he was in a car which was not fit to be on the road. It was a real hazard to all other drivers on the highway.

R.C.M.P. Officer: My gosh b'y! this car is a menace, and you are a menace to be driving a car in this condition. What about if you were coming down that steep hill over there and your brakes gave out?

Driver: Never mine 'bout dat b'y, me brudder 'll be driving 'er den.

JOE'S WISH

Some years ago we had a chap who did a lot of chores for our family. He was always available except when he earned a little too much money the day before and that meant he was in a position to buy a little too much beer.

His fondness for all alcoholic beverages upset his home life to the extent that his wife and children moved out. This made Joe very bitter as the following episode will attest.

One morning my sister-in-law engaged Joe in a conversation about marriage. Eventually he finished the discussion by proclaiming, "Mrs. Clouston, when I first married me wife, I loved her so much I could've eat her. NOW, I wish to God I had."

A VISITOR IN THE CONGREGATION

A minister abruptly finished his sermon by saying, "I'm sorry I have to terminate my sermon at this point. I had more to say but this morning when I went into my study to pick up the notes for my sermon, I discovered several pages were missing. Our dog had chewed them up."

The service was over and the minister was in the vestibule by the door and as usual was chatting with the members of his congregation as they came out of the church.

A visitor approached the minister and asked, "Pardon me Reverend, but does your dog have any pups? I would like to have one for our minister."

HOW FAR IS — EVER SO FAR?

In the spring of the year, there has been many occasions when the arctic ice has drifed in on the east coast. At such times, fishermen go out looking for seals and there have been times when the wind has changed and the ice has been blown out from shore and the men have been stranded. I have often heard of men being lost on the ice.

On one of these occasions, men were missing for four or five days but were found and rescued. When a number of fellows were discussing the situation and how they became lost on the ice, one of the older men piped up with this outburst:

"Dere's nuttin' to gitten' loosed on d'hice deese days. Sur dey sans out one of dem eeliocopters and 'ooks on t' ya an' carry's ya 'ome. Should a been long we twenty year ago. We drift mose to Hingland."

"Now, Skipper, you didn't drift to England!"

"Well, we drift ever-so-far."

"And how far is that?"

"Well, d'firse day hout, we drift one 'ell of a distance and the second day hout, we drift so far agin an' d'tird day when the sun come opp, eh come opp inside me."

73

UNLAWFUL FOOD

The Rev. Montgomery was, at one time, a Moravian Missionary on the Labrador coast. He was a very good friend of mine and he told me this true story.

One morning a chap associated with the mission shot a goose out of season. The goose was plucked, gutted, dressed and found itself in the oven in short order.

It was quite normal for the R.C.M.P. officer when visiting Makkovik to have dinner with us at the mission. On this very day that we shot the goose out of season, the R.C.M.P. officer came to Makkovik and as usual was asked to stay to dinner.

The goose was removed from the oven, carved and portioned to each one sitting at the table. The R.C.M.P. officer was asked to say the blessing. He did, and said as follows:

"We thank thee Lord for this unlawful food, amen."

Nothing more was said about the goose shot out of season.

LAUGHING AT OURSELVES

I don't tell Newfie Jokes very often but some are just plain funny. When I tell these two stories to Newfoundland audiences, they get a great laugh from them.

Two Newfoundlanders decided to go in business together on a fifty-fifty basis. They agreed on buying a truck and went to Prince Edward Island. They bought taties for $3.50 a barrel and came back to Newfoundland and sold them for $3.50 a barrel.

After one or two trips, one of the partners turned to his buddy and said, "B'y, we got to give this up. We're not makin' any money at this." At which the other exploded, "YEAH, I TOLD YA WE SHOULDA BOUGHT A BIGGER TRUCK."

Talking to Lew Marks, my brother-in-law who lives in the Codroy Valley, he told me that just before Christmas 1976, he was in a barber shop in Port-aux-Basques. A fellow in the shop, who had been a passenger on the ferry yesterday, told about a fellow traveller who kept saying, "Santa Claus had to be a Newfoundlander". Eventually one of the passengers took him up on it and said, "Why?" The reply, "Cuz he comes down through the chimney and there's two doors in the house."

GLASS-EYED

Back in the days when breathalyzer readings were not part and parcel of every impaired driving prosecution, an interesting drama was enacted in a Newfoundland courtroom.

A police witness rhymed off the usual list of complaints: "The accused's breath smelled of alcohol, his speech was thick and his eyes appeared glassy."

Defense counsel pointed out that there was no evidence as to how much his client had had to drink. He also demonstrated that the accused man's normal speech was rather thick. Then he turned to his client and said, "I believe you have something you'd like to show the court."

The man took out his glass eye and made a big production out of polishing it.

Game over for the Crown: a big victory for the defense.

WORTHWHILE OPINION

A henpecked Newfoundland husband was silent, as he watched his wife prepare to mount a very large picture of her mother on the living room wall.

"I simply can't decide the best place to put this picture of mother," she said, "I don't suppose you have a worthwhile opinion?"

"Well, I think hanging is too good for her," he replied.

THE NEWFIE BULLET

The Newfie Bullet is the name the Americans gave, during the Second World War, to our Newfoundland train, "The Express". It crossed Newfoundland once every twenty four hours. Eastward bound twenty four hours, westward bound twenty four hours. . . 550 miles each way.

After Confederation, the Canadian National Railways took the system over and after about twenty years, when they could not stand the expense of this pace any longer, they discarded our "Bullet". "What a revoltin' development!" "Yes, and what a revoltin' development when you try to travel on that train-replacin' bus line."

Anyway, the story I like about the "Bullet" is this conversation as follows:

Lady traveller in top berth to male traveller in lower berth -

LADY: "Would you mind gettin' out and gettin' me a blanket. I'm wunaful cold."

MALE: "Are you married?"

LADY: "No, I'm not married."

MALE: "How would you like to make out you are married?"

LADY: "Oh, I'd like that! That would be fun."

MALE: "WELL, GET OUT AND GET YOUR OWN BLASTED BLANKET!"

BANANAS

A woman came home from the supermarket and as her husband came into the kitchen, he could not believe it, bananas were everywhere.

Husband: What are you doing with all these bananas?

Wife: Well, they were on sale—all you wanted for a dollar. So I bought $3.00 worth.

THE CHALLENGER

Mr. Block, a member of a sports club where many outdoor activities took place, was continually boasting and blustering about his physical abilities.

A new member, Russ, got tired of hearing this fellow going on about what his capabilities were and he challenged the great Mr. Block. He said "Mr. Block I'll bet you that I can wheel something in a wheelbarrow from this clubhouse to the gate and you can't wheel it back."

Mr. Block looked the little fellow over and said, "OK Russ I'll take you up on that."

Many of their fellow members were looking on and Russ was smiling mischievously. A wheelbarrow was brought to the clubhouse steps.

Rubbing his hands in great glee, Russ grasped the handles of the wheelbarrow, motioned to Mr. Block and said, "Alright. Get in."

Judge Seamus O'Reagan of the Provincial Court of Newfoundland was present in court in St. John's when one of the town drunks was convicted of three offences under the Intoxicated Persons Act,

RIGHT ON

A middle aged man was about to have a heart transplant. The evening before the operation, the chief surgeon visited his patient and said, "Now, Michael, you are a very fortunate fellow. This is most unusual but you are to have a choice of three hearts. One is from a beautiful blonde, who has won a number of beauty contests, or a heart from a nuclear physicist, who has accomplished a lot in his work, or a heart from a banker, a banker who has gone from sweeping the floor to being the President. You have the night to think it over."

In the morning the surgeon returned. "Well, Michael, have you made your choice?" Michael replied, "Yes doctor, the banker." "Why the banker?" asked the doctor. To which Michael answered, "'Tis highly probable, it's never been used."

SELF-INFLICTED

Many service clubs have after-dinner speakers from time to time.

I have been a member of the Kinsmen Club for many years. About 1951, a year or so after Confederation in Newfoundland, Dr. Leonard Miller came to our club to speak to us and gave us some idea of the Government Health Plans which were being suggested. At one point in his talk he said if a certain plan was implemented, it would pay for everything except maternity. One of our members asked:

"Why not maternity, Dr. Miller?"

And before Dr. Miller could answer, a member of our club, lawyer Bill Adams, yelled out:

"BECAUSE 'TIS SELF-INFLICTED."

WHAT'S SUFFICIENT?

In a certain area of Newfoundland, about twenty years ago, it was necessary to expropriate land for a government project. Some of the land owners were quite disturbed over losing their land. It was decided to have a meeting in the school house with a government official to explain and discuss the problems arising.

The official talked for a considerable time and now and then he would say that there was no need to worry that everyone would get sufficient for their land. Then he stopped to ask if there were any questions and the following ensued:

ONLY POSSIBLE

A young fellow in the outports asked a visiting clergyman, "can I live a good Christian life on $70.00 a week?" "My boy," was the reply, "that's all you can."

WOULDN'T WE ALL FEEL THE SAME?

One of the best examples of folklore humour is an incident I experienced myself. Now, most of us at one time or another, through poor communication or for some other reason, have not been able to obtain the information we needed in order to proceed farther.

This fellow was in this very same position. On a visit to the Grace General Hospital one morning last year, I was waiting for a taxi. A man entered the hospital and I could see he was not in familiar surroundings, probably his first visit.

He approached the information desk and spent a minute or so talking with the receptionist. When he left her I could see he had not been enlightened by her answers. He walked along the corridor entering two offices and returning again to the corridor looking just as puzzled.

Eventually he went to the emergency desk and somehow the lady there and himself got on the same wave length. She stood up and coming towards me led the man so far, and then pointed to the elevator.

I had never seen this fellow before but I felt for him, and I was about to speak to him when he stopped in front of me and let his frustration explode with, "Ol' Man if I don't soon find d'feller I'm lookin' fer, ME WOUNDS WILL BE ALL' EALED".

PROTESTANTS ARE HONEST?

Many years ago Father Coady in Tor's Cove purchased while in St. John's two bottles of rum. He placed them on the back seat of his car but when he went to take them out when he arrived back home there was only one bottle there. He exclaimed,

A CRASH COURSE IN TRUCK DRIVING

Here is a joke that I recently heard, laughed at, and thought really funny. Anyway, here it is:

Two Newfoundlanders, Bill and Joe, went up to Toronto to look for work. After searching for days without any luck, they came across an ad in the *Toronto Star* which read as follows:

WANTED: TWO TRUCK DRIVERS TO DRIVE LONG DISTANCE. ONE TO REST WHILE THE OTHER DRIVES, AND VICE-VERSA.

Off the two of them went for an interview.

Bill went into the office first and after the manager found out he had all the qualifications, he got the first job, then Joe went in and he got the second job because he had the same qualifications as Bill.

The manager was interested in how Joe would react to emergency circumstances, so he put some situations to him and he passed the test . . . until the manager said, "Joe, if you were going down a mile-long hill at 70 mph and a long train started to cross the road, and you apply both your cab and trailer brakes to slow her down but nothing happens, what would you do?"

"I'd call Bill," said Joe.

"But why would you call Bill?" asked the manager.

"Well," said Joe, "Tis like this: Bill never saw a big accident in his life."

2½ lb. BABY

One morning one of my salesmen, Victor Westcott, came to my office and told me he wished to relate something that happened yesterday which was Sunday.

He had been to Placentia to visit his aunt who was in her 80's, rather invalided, but still quite bright and had not lost her wonderful sense of humour.

Victor had been married a couple of years and his aunt knew there was a baby due so she asked the question.

AUNT: "Victor, did Floss have the baby yet?"

VICTOR: "Yes, Aunt."

AUNT: "And how heavy was it?"

VICTOR: "2½ lbs., Aunt."

AUNT: "Oh, Victor, hardly worth havin', was it?"

ONE FROM MOSEY MURRIN

All communities in Newfoundland have what we term 'characters', fellows who are ever-ready with their fun and wit. I've heard a number of stories told about a character by the name of Mosey Murrin in Corner Brook.

I was told recently that on one occasion a local clergyman saw Mosey coming up the street and when Mosey was abreast of the priest he said, "Good morning Mosey."

"Good morning Fauder," he says.

"There's not much between you and a fool, is there Mosey?"

"No Fauder," says Mosey, "only the fence!"

BIBLE NAMES

The visiting evangelist had preached for nearly an hour and a half. He had gone through the prophets in the Old Testament and talked about them one by one. Suddenly he said:

"AND NOW WE COME TO JEREMIAH. WHAT WILL WE DO WITH JEREMIAH?" A man in the back row stood up and said, "HE CAN HAVE MY SEAT REVEREND. I'M JUST ABOUT TO LEAVE."

DR. CHASE'S OINTMENT

My friend, Bob MacLeod, made several trips around our island with Mr. Gerald S. Doyle in his yacht. By accompanying Gerald Doyle, Bob met many Newfoundlanders who told him some funny stories.

Bob visited one old gentleman, and while sitting in his kitchen, he was yarning with him. This gentleman knew that one of Gerald Doyle's agencies was Dr. Chase's products. Rather secretly he said to Bob, "Huncle Bob, b'y, dat Dr. Chase's hointment, dat's some good! I'ad a wart 'ere on me nick, 'an I wuz smearin' 'n on for mose a mont'. An', Huncle Bob, b'y, 'twas jus so well ya scratched yer hass wid a brick!"

DID YOU EVER GO TO SCHOOL?

I think that back, say fifty or sixty years ago, people were not frowned upon if they did not go to school. It surely proved quite a handicap in later years no doubt, but was not looked upon as a disgrace. His or her education was along practical lines, the kind that would bring income to the family unit now, be that income ever so small.

Some years after Confederation, Ottawa personel were interviewing older citizens of our island province. These people were endeavouring to find out how far reaching our illiteracy was. Now some people have a hard time answering questions with one or two words. Their answer has to be in the form of a story, short or long.

One gentleman to be interviewed was a survivor of the Newfoundland Disaster of 1914. He was the late Mr. Cecil Mouland. He told this story himself.

Interviewer: Mr. Mouland, how long were you in school?

Mr. Mouland: Well now zir, the first day I was in school they were readin' 'bout Tom and his dog. Someone threw a stick out into the pond, and Tom's dog went after it. Before Tom's dog was back to shore I was out of school.

A DOG'S LIFE

Dear Uncle Al,

"Recently I came across this ad in the *Calgary Sun*. I hope you see it as funny as I do.

"**Lost Dog: Faded brown, three legs, one ear missing, blind in left eye. Answers to the name LUCKY.**

"Hope it is good for another laugh. We enjoy your column very much."

84

THE WIT OF THE ELEVATOR GIRL

April 1, 1949, Confederation with Canada became a fact, Newfoundland became the tenth province of Canada.

During the first week of Confederation, quite a number of salesmen from Toronto and Montreal were in St. John's trying to drum up business for their respective companies.

It was the fifth day, a very wet, foggy, cold afternoon. ("Mauzie day" is the term in Newfoundland.) Six very unsuccessful and dejected salesmen had returned to the Newfoundland Hotel. In the elevator, one remarked,

85

SO WHAT?

The following is supposed to be an authentic story from the Northern Peninsula.

A tourist drove up to the gas station and requested $5.00 worth of gas. When the gas started to flow onto the ground the tourist called out, "Hey! The gas is running onto the ground."

Young tank attendant: "Yes, but 'tis not $5.00 worth yet."

UGLINESS

Visiting Port-aux-Basques last year to take part in the Lions dinner for Senior Citizens, I got involved with some very funny characters.

They told me of an actual conversation which took place in the lounge last Saturday. It appears that two fellows were talking disparagingly about the other's family. It was all in humour though. It got around to ugliness.

One exclaimed: "Your sister was so ugly they had to tie a couple of lamb chops around her neck to get the dogs to chase her."

The other said, "Me zon, you were so ugly when you were born that they had to go next door and borrow a baby to get you christened."

WHERE ARE THOSE PLACES?

It had been a great night of laughter, and it makes things go well if people can laugh without effort. On this occassion a lady came up to me and paid me the most unusual compliment by saying, "My H'Uncle Al, I've a laughed in places tonight I've never laughed before."

GOD LIVES IN STRANGE PLACES

A Sunday School superintendant asked all the gathering of children, where does God live?

He received no reply for several seconds and then one young fellow ventured,

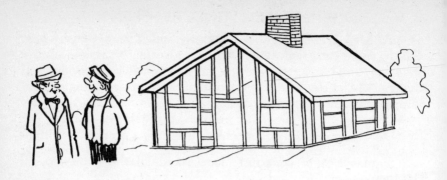

A chap from Port-de-Grave was asked "So youse buillding a new 'ouse! 'ows it comin?"

"First rate. I've got the roof and mortgage on, and I spects to have the furnace and sherriff in before fall."

A RED LIGHT MEANS?

A nurse in St. John's was hurrying to be on duty by the prescribed time of 4:00 P.M. She was driving faster than usual and had beaten two red lights. The third light proved her downfall. The light was yellow alright but went red just as she entered the intersection.

It took only a few seconds and when she looked in the mirror, yes sir, there he was right on her bumper with his revolving red light flashing. She pulled to the curb and it was not long before he was asking for her license.

She produced the licence as he said, Policeman: Do you know what a red light means? Nurse: Yes! Someone wants the bed pan.

GOOD NIGHT

A few years ago a well-known gentleman in one of the small outports, who was an eligible bachelor, made a practice of visiting a widow who lived close by, every evening and had tea with her.

A friend of the gentleman in question suggested that he should marry the lady. "I have often thought about it," he said, "but where would I spend my evenings then?"

LONG HAS TWO DIMENSIONS

An Island Cove man had a contract to build a house in St. John's. The necessary lumber was supposed to be on the site but after a few days he ran short of two by fours. He proceeded to Horwood Lumber Co. to obtain the extra stock. Being a good H'Island Cove feller he had to have some fun so when he was asked what he wanted he announced that he needed one hundred four by two's. The clerk corrected him and said he wanted two by four's. An argument broke out on the subject as follows:

ANGELS FLY?

"Do angels fly mother?"

"Yes dear."

"Then when is nursie going to fly, cause Daddy called her angel last night."

"I can tell you now, she'll fly tomorrow."

NO OTHER ALTERNATIVE

Before the days of automobiles and trucks, all Her Majesty's mail was carried by water to various areas of our coast. Settlements which were accessible by horse and wagon received theirs in this alternate manner. The Southern Shore was one of these areas, and mail and newspapers only went up the shore twice or three times a week.

A story which I was told originated in Ferryland and goes like this: A man went into the general store and made an announcement in very loud and direct terms—

Customer: I wants d'newspaper.

Owner: Do y'want yisteidy's or t'days?

Customer: I wants t'days.

Owner: Well, y'll have t'wait 'til tamarra.

LUMBER IN THE ATTIC

A Newfoundlander had just completed a new house. He had gone to the beer parlour to socialize with a few friends.

After he had been there for a couple of hours, someone rushed in and said,

91

A HAPPENING DURING THE SECOND WORLD WAR

From time to time people have sent me stories of humour from all over Newfoundland.

One kind lady in Curling has sent me many humourous stories but also has included some stories of which are not of humour but make excellent interesting reading. I have decided to include some of them in this publication.

Some of them are ghost stories and you will find them here and there throughout the book. This lady was brought up on the Grey Islands.

Here is one story.

The second year of World War Two one muggy night in early fall a group of us were sitting on Uncle Bernard's front gallery. We were chatting and laughing and also listening to the night sounds and to us the war seemed so far away. The tide was low and a small fog bank had moved into the outer edge of the harbour beyond us.

Suddenly from out of this fog bank loomed a large fire-ball and sparks flew everywhere. We stood in amazement, then ran for the landwash across the meadow. Just as we reached the beach, this fire-ball came out of the fog bank again and sent us reeling back in the other direction. "The Phantom" we said, but there was also a war on.

There were numerous submarines in the Straits of Belle Isle, but then a sub could not get that close near shore among the breakers. I felt myself it may have been "that old buccaneer up to his hi-jinks again. But we'll never know what it really was. Flares? Maybe.

But it's embedded in my memory and I can still see the sparks fly.

Jean Hurley
Grey Islands

WOULD YOU BELIEVE IT?

Visiting with some friends one evening I was happy to find myself in the company of a married couple from Notre Dame Bay. I found their company very pleasant and entertaining.

The wife told some humourous stories from their lives, things that actually happened. The one I found most humourous was from their courting days.

The story is that in their courting days they lived in Notre Dame Bay but in two outports six miles apart. Transportation was such that Jack had to walk the six miles four times a week to see his intended Flossie. On his way he always dropped in to see his friend Mickey, who lived very close to Jack's own house.

On one particular evening Jack made his visit to Mickey's and after a short stay proceeded on his way as usual. He was gone about an hour and a half when he appeared again at Mickey's. Mickey looked at Jack rather surprised saying, "What's happend Jack, you were here once before this evening"? Suddenly Jack appeared to come to his senses and exclaimed "OH MY GOSH! I turned around to put me back to the wind to light me pipe and forgot to turn around again".

His wife confirmed the story saying, "That was one night I wasn't very much on his mind".

INTELLIGENT FELLOW

This story is told about an incident which took place during a session of the circuit court.

The defending lawyer had been receiving very little co-operation from a witness. He paced back and forth wondering how to stop the witness from giving evasive answers, and then he turned on him quickly,

LAWYER: "Do you know any fellows on this jury?"

WITNESS: "Yes, zar, more den 'alf of dem."

LAWYER: "Well now, at last we are getting some helpful information. Are you willing to swear that you know more than half of the men on this jury?"

WITNESS: "Well now, zar, if its any help to ya, I'm willin' to swear I knows more den all dem put togedder."

A WHEELBARROW FULL

We calls 'em Mainlanders, and this one had been looking around the cove trying to buy a piece of land. He had talked to quite a few of the people but when they discovered that he wanted it for almost a gift he did not have much success.

Eventually he came to the remotest area of the community and tried to be pleasant enough.

The conversation dragged a bit at one point and he said to the local land owner, "I'd like to buy five hundred dollars worth of land from you."

"Good," said the local, "that's very good. Go get your wheelbarrow and I'll fill it up for you."

ALL HE GOT WAS NAR CHRISTMAS!

Some years ago in the month of January I met a friend on Water Street who had spent Christmas on the Burin Peninsula.

He said that one afternoon he was in a shop and was listening to two old fellas yarnin'.

Suddenly one said, "Look at 'n, dere's Joe comin' dere. Eh's a fullish feller, went h'off an' joined Jehovers Witness. Wonder what eh got outa dat."

The other replied, "I allow ol' man all eh got outa dat, wuz nar Christmas!"

Halfway down a steep hill near Bay de Verde, the strangers stopped their car to ask if the hill was dangerous.

SWEARING

A story which was told to me by the Rev. Len Ludlow was about a boatman whom he employed one time. The Reverend told me that this fellow had a bad habit of swearing. It did not matter who reprimanded him, the fellow kept on.

One particular evening, they were steaming up St. Anthony harbour and there were quite a number of vessels laying at anchor. He could see them all quite well in the twilight, silhouetted against the horizon.

As he steamed along, suddenly he realized there was a large vessel bearing right down upon his boat. He knew there was no chance of avoiding a collision, and sure enough there was an awful smack when the larger vessel hit his boat right amidships.

The Reverend was sure they would capsize. But they didn't. His boat was leaking badly, and both the boatman and himself were thoroughly shaken up, but no injuries.

Things were right silent and nobody said a word, when the reverend came up with the following: "SAY, JACK, THERE MUST BE SOMETHING WRONG, YOU DIDN'T SWEAR?" The boatman replied, "Well, to tell you the truth, Reverend, I thought it would be a good chance for you."

THE COW

It was in June of 1975 and my record "Spinnin' Yarns" had just been placed on the market. Wanting to publicize the fact, I parcelled up a record for Barbara Frum and Allan Maitland and left them at the office of "As It Happens" in the C.B.C. building in Toronto. I was visiting there so I indicated my Toronto phone number. I said to myself, "If this is good humour, they will be getting in touch with me." Sure enough, the next afternoon, Beverley Reid, their top researcher, phoned and invited me to come and be interviewed on "As It Happens" that evening.

Barbara and Allan treated me very kindly. I think they are two grand people. All three of us had a great laugh, and from what I heard, the radio audience did also.

During the interview, Barbara put this question to me, "Al, what do you think of the Newfie jokes?" I replied, "Barbara, most of them are very silly, but there's a few I like."

"Have you heard a good one lately?" I said, "Yes", and I continued,

Two fellows were talking about their respective wives and one had given his wife quite a buildup and finished with . . .

HIGHWAY # 27

In June 1975, I was the mayor of the Newfoundland Pavilion at the Toronto Caravan.

Looking for more publicity for my record, "Spinnin' Yarns", I was successful in getting on a number of T.V. and radio shows.

Betty Kennedy very kindly granted me an interview on her afternoon show. When I was asked by my friends what Betty Kennedy was really like, I said this: "If you had a cousin and you had heard a lot of nice things about her but had never met her, then suddenly you did meet her and found they were all true, that is all I can say about Betty Kennedy.

Anyway, as always, the topic of the Newfie jokes was discussed at this interview. I said too many of these jokes were very silly, but I did tell her this one.

A Newfoundlander was in his car on the Ontario highway. He was driving at the one speed, not a mile over nor under. The Ontario Provincial Police came by and motioned at him to pull over. The officer questioned him and asked to see his licence, then said, "Can't this car go any faster? You got all the traffic held up in this lane. You'll have to go faster." The Newfoundlander said, "What's wrong with you; look at all the signs, 27, 27, 27", and the police officer bellowed, "OH, MY GOSH! I'M GLAD I GOT TO YOU BEFORE YOU GOT ON THE 401."

CLOSE TO HEAVEN BY CAR

A typical example of folklore humour is the following story. I was requested in May this year to give an entertainment at HL. Breton which is on the Sou'wess coast of Newfoundland.

The lady I stayed with, Rosie Strickland, told me about an older man who bought a car. He had never had a licence to drive a car before this, and people were rather reluctant to ride with him.

Eventually, a friend who was feeling sorry for the new driver, decided to accompany him on one occasion, when the friend was asked whether or not he was nervous he replied, "Well, I tell ya now. When he got her up to 50, I was singing 'ABIDE WITH ME'. When he got her up to 70 I sang 'NEARER MY GOD TO THEE' and when he got her up to 90 I sang, 'LORD I'M COMING HOME'.

A fellow being interviewed up along on the mainland was asked . . .

A MILLION LAUGHS

Hi Uncle Al,

This is a joke told by a contestant on Groucho Marx's show I've seen years ago. It goes like this:

An old man, who had a ticket on a lottery, won a million dollars but his wife and daughter were afraid to tell him, afraid the shock might kill him. They decided to call in their priest and said, "Father, we want you to tell Dad that he won a million dollars, but tell him in such a way that the shock won't kill him."

The priest agreed and proceeded to talk to the old man. Eventually he said, "I understand you had a ticket on the lottery."

The old man said, "Yes Father, I did."

"Now then," asked the priest, "what would you do if you won a million dollars?"

"Well Father," said the old man, "if I won a million dollars, I'd give you half."

The priest dropped dead.

Sadie Moriarty
Harbour Grace

IT MADE NO DIFFERENCE

A very good friend of mine, a professor at the Memorial University, told me about a new professor who came to the University in September, 1978.

Anne Marie was in his own classes for two years. She was one girl who never failed to express herself without making very clear what she meant.

When our new professor was only there ten days he stopped when he was halfway through his lecture and said, "Am I going too fast?" Anne Marie spoke up and replied, "Don't worry about it prof. 'Tis not worth slowin' up for".

UNCLE JOHN HAD LIGHT AFTER DEATH

The Lions Club of Bloomfield-Musgravetown had a birthday party at which I was invited to speak.

Before I left Bloomfield a gentleman related the following story.

He explained that when the various communities around Newfoundland were being electrified, not every one could afford to have their house wired. A common thing for them to say was, "they couldn't afford to get the lights in."

An old man died down in Bunion's Cove and two men were engaged to dig the grave. Before they finished their digging it became dark. They arranged with a man living near the graveyard and close to the grave site, to bring a wire from his house so they could keep digging and finish the job before they went home. Another old gentleman saw the light down in the graveyard and said to himself,

SIMPLE THINKING THOUGH DISASTROUS

An alcoholic, who had a long and varied experience with the stuff, decided for himself to seek some help. He went to his regular physician who knew this patient very well.

First of all the doctor gave him a considerable amount of advice. Then he gave the man a complete physical examination to discover what inroads the alcohol had made on its victim over the years. When the interview had started the doctor felt the man's hearing was noticeably impaired and on examination he confirmed for himself that this was true. So the doctor advised him that if he didn't stop drinking he would go completely deaf.

Six months went by before our patient made his next visit to his doctor. The man's hearing had become considerably worse. So with some impatience the doctor said to him, "Look here Harry, can't you do better than this and try to give up your drinking? I told you you would go deaf."

And Harry's reply was, "Well, Doc b'y, I'll tell ya d'way it is. I likes what I drinks more den what I hears."

➤

A TOUGH BUDGET

Uncle Joe was always asked his opinion on just about anything that the Municipal Council or the government was up to.

The budget for the city of Corner Brook had just been published that afternoon. Leaning over the fence that evening he was asked what in his opinion was the most interesting item in the budget. Well, he felt that the most interesting thing to him was the fact that the Humber River was only going to run twice a week.

GLOSSARY

'Arn	Horn	Postal	Posts and Telegraphs
'Arse	Horse	Put to Rights	Put in Order
Bate	Beat		
Bid	Bed	Rightly Mind	Remember
B'y	Boy	Saun	Send
Cartny	Certainly	Scoff	A Plentiful Meal
Clue Up	To Conclude, Finish		
Cuffer	Chat or Talk	Settle	Couch
		Short Order	Very Little Time
D'ead	The Head		
Deah	Dear	Sot	Sit
Dere	There	Taties	Potatoes
Dere's	There is	Taucht	Thought
'Ead	Head	Teen	Thin
Ee	He	T'ick	Thick
Feesh	Fish	T'in	Thin
Full of a Glitter	Covered with Ice	Toime	Time, Meaning a Party
Gisen	Give Him		
Gonna	Going to	Waz or Wuz	Was
Heft	Lift	Weem	We are
Iddn't	Is Not	Wee'n	With Him
'Long We	Along with Us	Whaze	What is
		Wick	Week
Mose	Most	Wunerful	Wonderful
Nar	Neither	Wunts	Wants
Nerra	Neither	Zar or Zir	Sir
Piller	Pillow	You'm	You are
		Youse	You
		Yees	You